What Solo-profession About This Book...

*"**Personal Brand Clarity**, highlighted what has been missing when it comes to understanding how I differentiate my coaching business, to focus on my brand, not my website and logo. I now have a greater understanding of what value positioning means and the advantage I have in creating content that competitively distinguishes me from my competitors. The exercises, examples, and insight Suzanne provided are significant to the growth of my fellow entrepreneurs as well as leaders in any organization. The confidence I have gained, in recognizing and owning my brand, has shown up in my personal relationships as well guiding me as I step into my potential as I grow my business!"*

- Melissa Healy, National Certified Wellness Coach, Melissa Healy Wellness Coaching

*"The process in **Personal Brand Clarity** is simple, but not easy! The brilliant exercises require a deep dive into the core of who you are. If you are not willing to go there, then you are not willing to grow! I committed to doing this work, and am reaping the benefits ever since. The clarity of knowing my personal brand's value position is a game-changer in how I lead my staff and other employees, and how I deliver my expertise every day. I highly recommend this book and program to every leader out there!"*

- Liz Killen-Scott, Vice President of Organizational Development & Engagement, Ent Credit Union

Endorsements continued...

*"I loved creating my Personal Brand Style attributes in this process. Just by identifying and defining them, I am now able to make them more tangible and become more of me, unabashedly! As an Independent Distributor for an international company, this process has given me the clarity to take action and feel more confident to further my distinction and expertise on what I can bring to my clients, and others in my circle of influence. My personal brand really does rock! And **Personal Brand Clarity**, is helping me to bring it to life!"* — **Katie Sevenants,** Independent Distributor, Senegence International

*"**Personal Brand Clarity** is so much more than a solopreneurial business branding book, it is a book that guides you to become more of who you know yourself to be in EVERY facet of your life. Suzanne painlessly and thoroughly guides you through her proven process to uncover the attributes of your unique Personal Brand Presence DNA that becomes yours to step into fully. And when you do, the clarity causes doors to start opening up as you become more & more aligned. The insights you will gain will stay with you for years to come, I promise! I highly recommend this book and program to all my entrepreneurial friends before you spend more money in marketing!"* — **Julie Miller Davis,** CEO & Founder JMD Productivity Training

"Too often we look outside of ourselves for the answers to more esteem, self-confidence, a better life, and happiness. But until we realize that all of that will come with the clarity we get around who we are, we just keep spinning our wheels searching for it. Personal Brand Clarity guides the reader to uncover and define who they truly know themselves to be, and then to step into it with a higher level of consciousness. When YOU are clear, your customers and prospects are too!" - **Regina Clarke,** *Brainwave Balancing*

PERSONAL BRAND CLARITY

*Identify, Define & Align
to What You Want to Be Known For*

By Suzanne Tulien

Brand Clarity Expert

BRAND ASCENSION PUBLISHING

**Personal Brand Clarity / Identify, Define, & Align
to What You Want to Be Know For.**

ISBN: 978-0-9818275-1-3 (paperback)
ISBN: 978-0-9818275-2-0 (hard cover)
  BUS107000   **BUSINESS & ECONOMICS** / Personal Success SEL027000
  SELF-HELP / Personal Growth / Success

Cover and Interior Design/Layout by Suzanne Tulien.

QUANTITY PURCHASES: Colleges, companies, professional groups, clubs, and other organizations may qualify for special terms, and/or quantity discounts of this title. For information, email inquiry@Brandascension.com.

Printed in the United States of America.

CONTENTS

ACKNOWLEDGEMENTS

First and foremost, I must thank all the thought leaders who have disrupted the norms, continued to question our own evolution as we know it, who keep digging deeper, and invited all of us to get more conscious, strategic, and deliberate in our own personal development. From enterprises and movements like Vishen Lakhiani's MindValley, to Esther Hicks/Abraham-Hicks, Deepak Chopra, Ekhart Tolle, Dr. Bruce Lipton, and Oprah Winfrey's ever evolving depth into self-improvement, I could not have begun the delightful ongoing process of expanding into my potential without the sharing of all this profound knowledge and your tenacity to teach others what you know.

I believe the core of our evolution and overall survival as a society lies deep within our own understanding of ourselves first. With the belief that everything begins from the "inside-out," I set out to apply that to business operations as well as the individual self.

My second book (co-written), *Brand DNA – Uncover Your Organization's Genetic Code for Competitive Advantage,* revealed a process for companies and their teams to identify, define and align to a set of meaningful constructs that they could adhere to, make tangible, and stand for, thus creating a "gestalt" set of perceptions for their targeted markets to know and love. It was with the development of this methodology, that enabled my co-author and business partner at that time, Carol Chapman, and I to dive into years of practical application and prove its power. And I am truly grateful for that incredible experience.

But none of this would have evolved if it weren't for my amazing clients who also had a deep desire for clarity and inherently knew this process would benefit their own evolution in so many facets of their lives. They trusted the process, and I am eternally grateful for that. Since inception, I have seen countless success stories, awareness breakthroughs, and more generative journeys towards their own evolution, over and over again. And with that success, was the inspiration to reach out to the solopreneurial and leadership focused individuals who keep their hearts and minds on the bigger picture of growth and expansion for themselves and the people they serve.

Thank you also to those who have come into my life at "just the right time" (the Universe is truly amazing) to support my efforts in moving forward, taking strategic risks, trusting my gut, and having more fun doing what I love.

Specifically, in this book project, Camille Parker, of Carerra Ink, for her expertise in editing, organizing, and refining the structure of my "download" of information I chose to share in this book. And to my team at BookLaunchers.com who "up'd my game" with this 3rd book launch —I am so grateful for all your knowledge and expertise and teamwork! I am thrilled with its outcome and excited to deliver it to those who are ready for their next evolution, from the inside out.

DEDICATION

To every brave solo-professional who every day chooses to do what they love, being who they are, with a high level of consciousness, dedication, determination, and tenacity so that you can live your fullest potential and others can benefit from what they know.

And to my best friend, biggest cheerleader, husband, and very gentle, kind-hearted soul, Jon, for your love and support; I learn so much from you; I am forever in love with you and oh so grateful we found each other.

"Becoming the CEO of your life is a matter of becoming more conscious, strategic, & deliberate with WHO you are."

– Suzanne Tulien,
Brand Clarity Expert,
Brand Ascension

———

FOREWORD

If you are in business, then you have wasted money on marketing that did not properly define you, marketing that was wildly ineffective, and you probably also launched a marketing campaign that was ignored.

I know. I've wasted that money, too. Interestingly enough, when I need accounting help, I hire an accountant. When I need legal help, I find a great attorney. And somehow I thought I could do my own branding and my marketing. What was I thinking?

I do realize that over the years owning my companies, I have wasted money on false starts, branding ideas that never matured, and advertising that was not aligned with what I do and who I am as a leader and entrepreneur.

These are all rookie mistakes. This book is the cure.

Thankfully, I met Suzanne early in my career. She has helped me identify, define and align to not only my unique personal brand with my company but a personal brand presence within all facets of my life.

So, how do you differentiate yourself? How do you get noticed in a way that works in alignment with your own core values? We know that product differentiation is the key to product success. The difference is the 'magic.' Our personal branding is all about leveraging the magic we bring to the table. It is how we, as Suzanne always puts it, "*identify, define, and align to our authentic selves that naturally differentiates us from competition.*"

I don't know about you, but I want to enjoy the people I work with on a day-to-day basis. I want to look forward to our meaningful conversations. I want to attract and work with people who love serving others, radiate positivity, and who look forward to the future while enjoying the present. I want to love doing what I do and being authentic every single day. I think most of us do. In order to do that, we need to be more conscious and deliberate while leading through authenticity. It is an increased level of emotional intelligence about ourselves that builds the trust that exceeds not only our customer expectations but our own expectations for excellence. Great brand definition creates the clarity to do just that.

The inside-out process of Personal branding identifies and clarifies what we intrinsically know about ourselves and it enables us to confidently convey our brand value position to people who want and need to hear it.

Successful personal brands know that business happens when a buyer and a seller experiences a double coincidence of wants. I can hear Suzanne touting, *"Your marketing might get a prospect in the door, but it is your brand that turns them into a client and keeps them coming back."*

One of my favorite chapters in this book is chapter 5, called, "The Secret Power of Mantra and Knowing Your Why." This is all about how to attract the people you want to work with and for. Everyone is not your potential buyer. If you try to please everyone, you will wind up pleasing no one, including yourself. The clearer we are in knowing ourselves (our unique way of being), the easier it is to attract our perfect clients who appreciate our way of delivering of our expertise.

This book, and her Personal Brand Presence methodology helps us figure out, in both our personal and professional life, where we want to spend our resources and how we want to spend our time. An alignment that helps us to be accountable to our true selves.

Now more than ever, solo-professionals need to be reminded of why you do what you do. It's too easy to be discouraged when you're are not fully cognizant of your purpose. Personal Brand Clarity is written to help us figure out why you get out of bed, who you want to serve with a heart filled with gratitude, and in a way that exudes your joy for what you do. That's living fully in alignment!

Solo-professionals will find this compelling content and practical exercises invaluable, and leaders will make it mandatory reading for their teams to rise to their next personal elevation.

Congrats, Suzanne!

Mary C. Kelly, PhD, CSP, CPAE, Commander USN (retired)
Author, *Who Comes Next? Leadership Succession Planning Made Easy*

INTRODUCTION

Congratulations for investing into your full potential! You realize that you are the Brand of your business (and life for that matter) and have the power to create distinction through authenticity and clarity! I am so excited because I know you are in the right place!

If you are reading this right now, you have a curiosity about who you are and how you can begin to truly leverage what you know, how you show up, and what you can do more of to leave an impact on the world. This book is designed to enable you to realize what you bring to the table. I wrote it for the solo professional and leader-minded individual who is driven to expand and grow regularly and become more of who they really are. Why is that important for YOU? Because it satisfies the deepest of yearnings to know you are here for a reason.

By reading and completing the exercises in this book, you'll be able to clearly articulate the essence of who you are as a Personal Brand (we'll define that later). By doing so, you'll realize just how important it is to advance your strategic competitive advantage within your professional and personal life.

You'll also be well-positioned to leverage your Personal Brand Presence to:
- Ensure you create distinction in the minds of your audience, family, and friends, to become more memorable.
- Tap into your uniqueness in a highly consistent, engaging way that sets you apart.
- Stay committed to your authentic self by discerning differently, protecting what you stand for, and showcasing your Personal Brand's value position consistently to build trust and advocacy.

The work you do in these chapters and lessons gives you the unique perspective to see yourself and your business from the inside out. It is designed to take you to a new level of clarity and help uncover your Personal Brand's value position (a "knowing" of why you are here on this planet in this time and space), instill more confidence, and align yourself to thrive doing what you love. By completing this process, you are already 10 steps ahead of your competition in building a solid, unshakeable Personal Brand Presence foundation!

Shh! I'll tell you a secret...most entrepreneurs don't do this deep internal Brand development work, and that is to your advantage and distinction!

After nearly 16 years of being in the advertising, marketing, and communications industry, I cofounded Brand Ascension in early 2004. Brand Ascension is a consulting and training firm created to help companies (and now solo-professionals) get the clarity they need to identify, define, and align to their unique distinction, mission, and promise; to do what they love at the highest level of purpose consciousness possible.

At that time, I saw a void in the small business market for best practices in the area of internal Brand-building.

Most businesses focused on getting their products and services out there by being highly externally focused on strategies such as marketing and advertising. I spent hours studying the leading practices of successful Brands that created deep connections and loyal followings with their customers, but had started with a core understanding of their own value position, and created an internal values-driven culture of collaboration for the mission.

I discovered that these brands (i.e. Google, Ben & Jerry's, Tom's Shoes, Build-a-Bear, Disney, Starbucks, REI, to name a few) did several things differently, from the inside out, and we put these strategies into a simple step-by-step process to teach businesses not only to define their Brands but build and leverage them from the inside out.

I soon realized solo-preneurs weren't getting the clarifying information in a process that was practical and implementable, not to mention focused on their own authenticity. So, in 2011, I adapted our Brand DNA methodology to specifically help solo-professionals (non-employers), consultants, coaches, sales agents, brokers, speakers, and practitioners, and leaders, like you, to reach their potential through the clarity of their differentiation.

You might be wondering why I am so passionate about YOU and your success. Well, because I get it...

I was baby number three in my family of four siblings. You can Google countless articles from psychologists, parenting social workers, and the like to understand the effects of that birth order includes feeling left out, invisible, treated unfairly, with no real development of their own identity. It has been a journey-quest of mine since my early teens when I started realizing my individualistic characteristics, resisting conformity, and asking more philosophical, existential questions (without knowing what the word "existential" actually meant back then!).

To put more "icing on the cake" so to speak, I was enrolled in a Catholic school from first grade through eighth grade. From the strict, rote learning style of the nuns to the incessant bullying from other fear-driven students, I succumbed to the damage...for a long time until I got tired of not being happy, or inspired, motivated, and empowered. I was tired of the endless efforts to please others, when I myself was not happy.

You see, I sought others' approval for a long time. I wanted to be recognized, to "fit-in", to be loved, unconditionally. It was an underlying effort that didn't result in positive experiences — I couldn't figure out why I wasn't thriving.

One day, I came to the conclusion that I didn't really understand who I was. And I began to understand that when you are unsure, you are more manipulatable. I had leaned into what everything everybody else was and when I finally realized what I was doing, I was struck with curiosity and a "need to know" drive that led me to some amazing teachings about the state of the "human being" and our age-old quest to answer the question "Who Am I?"

When you uncover the DNA (Dimensional Nucleic Assets™ — the full authentic essence of YOU) that makes up your Personal Brand Presence (the truth about who you know yourself to be and how you deliver on it every day), you will begin to discern everything a bit differently and start aligning your actions and behaviors toward what makes you, YOU. This helps you be more proactive instead of reactive in building your business and life dreams, while creating more ease and flow into your overall experience. Being proactive at a highly conscious level keeps you in the "driver's seat" of your life and enables you to make focused decisions which are in alignment with who you really are, hence enabling the ability to manifest more things and situations that help to perpetuate your growth.

And you aren't going to be the only one who notices! Your customers will notice, your colleagues will notice, and your family and friends will notice the powerful focus you will have to leverage your full potential!

You are more powerful and valuable than you think!

Why this works...
So what is behind the power of recognizing your authentic Personal Brand Presence and empowering yourself to cocreate your desired life? It is related to a concept called The Pygmalion Effect (or the Rosenthal Effect) and the theory behind the "self-fulfilling prophecy" model. The name is derived from the mythical Greek character, Pygmalion, who had carved such a beautiful statue that he fell in love with it, so much so, that he eventually brought her to life.

In other words, Pygmalion's perception (belief) of this seemingly inanimate rock as a beautiful living woman changed its very physical nature into a beautiful human woman.

This fable's effect was popularized by an interesting scientific study that showed that teachers' perceptions of their students impacted their students' innate IQ level. When the teacher perceived a student as an "intellectual bloomer" (even if this held no measurable validity), that student became an intellectual bloomer. *Source: Rosenthal, R. and L. Jacobsen. Pygmalion in the classroom: teacher expectation and pupils' intellectual development. New York: Holt, Rinehart and Winston, 1968.*

The Pygmalion Effect then became a self-fulfilling prophecy. How we choose to perceive the people in our life brings those perceptions into reality. If that is true, then how we choose to perceive ourselves in life will bring those perceptions into our reality.

Bottomline: Your expectations influence your own performance. And the clearer you are about what you believe about yourself (your Personal Brand Presence), the more you enable yourself to become it.

One of my clients who was in the health industry as a massage therapist and although she loved her clients, she knew she could be doing more. She went through this process and realized she had been listening to a parent who regularly told her she wasn't smart enough to be a chiropractor (which was her real dream). This process gave her the clarity about herself, that infused confidence to continue the training to become a licensed chiropractor and is now, just a few years later, living her dream and creating a powerful value position in all facets of her life because of what she now knows is her value position and is clear and confident on what she stands for.

When you realize that your perceptions are actively collaborating with every part of your world, how you choose to perceive things is not simply a passive analysis of the past, it's an active integration of the present. And upon discovering the Truth about our innate power, our world turns into a cocreative possibility. Active, conscious integration is possible when you identify, define, and align yourself to your unique Personal Brand Presence. In other words, you cannot step into and become what you are unaware of. And the more aware you are of WHO you are, the more you can deliberately become it.

So there, let's do this!

"Your purpose in life is to find your PURPOSE, and LIVE it fully."

– Buddah

———

HOW TO GET THE MOST FROM THE PROCESS

This is not a race to be completed. Think of it as a journey to be savored in each present moment and reflected on. The more you relax into this journey, the more you will fully enjoy the intricacies of your uniqueness and allow them to bubble up to the surface, get acknowledged, and begin to take full flight.

Enjoy the journey of falling back in love with yourself.

Over the course of this book, gift yourself optimum space to walk through the ideas, insights and urge for changes that come to you. That means mark your calendar for uninterrupted time to focus on this work. You will be so glad you did!

Set up this time as special "me time" just for your next evolution. Take that deeper dive into knowing yourself and unlocking your confidence, clarity and superpowers that create your competitive advantage. It's ready to be recognized and nurtured!

Once you truly know and "own" your Personal Brand and align to it, the magic starts, the world opens up and begins working in your conscious, strategic, and deliberate favor!

Get ready, get focused, and get clear as you identify, define, and align with your unique Personal Brand Presence!

> **NOTE:** This book is not about MARKETING. It is the process that, ideally, comes BEFORE the marketing efforts. Here, you will be clarifying your unique value position that you would then use to *go to market, more consciously, strategically and deliberately*.

"Your level of success is inextricably related to your level of personal development."

– Claire Zammit, PhD, Evolving Wisdom, & Feminine Power Global Community

———

CHAPTER 1

YOUR PERSONAL BRAND PRESENCE IS IN YOUR DNA

Welcome to *PERSONAL BRAND CLARITY: How to Identify, Define & Align to What You Want to be Known For.*

I will be with you as you progress throughout this book with stories, examples, and key learning points to guide you along this clarifying journey.

I am excited to say the "PERSONAL BRAND PRESENCE" methodology has positively transformed hundreds of solo-professionals and leaders, just like you, in a variety of industries and life situations, equipping them with powerful tools to implement their unique Personal Brand to live their potential.

I appreciate how valuable your time is and I'd like to acknowledge and congratulate you on your efforts in carving out precious time to work on your Personal Brand. What you will experience throughout this book's teachings are the missing pieces that will help you dig deep to identify, define, and most importantly align to become a consciously consistent, distinctive, and engaging Personal Brand through your own unique Dimensional Nucleic Assets® (DNA).

This book was designed to transform the way you interpret yourself by providing you with thought-provoking, practical information you can begin using immediately to clarify and build out your Personal Brand through a fun and inspiring step-by-step, guided process! I guarantee you will get as much out of it as you put into it, so prepare to dig in!

1

I recommend you review each entire chapter in full, prior to getting into each specific lesson. Then move on to the next chapter. This is a process that builds upon itself so stay the course. Carving out a specific time each day or week is powerful in committing to do the work and reap all the benefits this clarity will provide you.

Upon completion of Chapter 1, you'll:
- Understand the true difference between the process of Personal/Business Brand-building vs. the process of Marketing efforts and function.
- Learn how you can take control of, manage, and elevate the perceptions others have of your Personal Brand Presence.
- Begin to define your unique Personal Brand Presence DNA attributes from within.
- Why your core Values are an essential tool to your individual success and authenticity.
- Identify and define your Personal Values to bring them into your consciousness so that you can activate their power from within.

As you can see, you are in for powerful teachings with this chapter and through the rest of the book. It is highly recommended you carve out at least one to two hours of uninterrupted time for these chapters... You may find you need more time to fully contemplate and reflect, so give yourself the gift of time when investing in your Personal Brand development!

It is important to kick start this learning by clarifying one of the biggest misunderstandings business owners have when deciding what to do to grow and expand. This is about realizing two primary functions that are foundational to business expansion: Branding and Marketing. Thus, Lesson 1 dives into these functions and helps you understand how each is separate, but divinely and strategically intertwined to enhance the value position and differentiation you develop in the minds of your perfect markets.

Are you ready to dive in? Let's get to it!

Lesson 1: Distinguishing Between Personal/Business Brand-Building vs. Marketing Activities

Did you know 73% of all businesses (23 million people as of this writing) are sole proprietorships/non-employers (*source: irs.gov/statistics, Spring 2019 reporting on Soleproprietor Returns, Tax Year 2016*).

Competition in any industry can be daunting, so that is why gaining clarity from Your Brand Within is so important for you! I know that building a Brand can be a confusing topic for many solo professionals, such as speakers, contractors, coaches, real estate agents, practitioners, distributors, consultants, brokers, and others, but stick with me.

After working through this process, you will become your own "Personal Brand Manager" equipped with my Brand "DNA framework' enabling you to take on-brand actions that will elevate you to your full alignment — and accelerate your growth by building an internal value proposition so you can exponentially and positively position your business and enable your life dreams to come to fruition!

As a savvy professional, I know you are reading this book because you understand the value of consistency, distinction, leadership and full on engagement with your circle of influence, from your family members, to your friends and colleagues as well as to your business clients. Your Personal Brand is not different from relationship to relationship. At its core, it is authentic, consistent, and intentional. Our goal together is to reveal those key attributes that help you self-actualize into these traits and live your potential!

If that is what you are looking for, well, congratulations, you are in the right place!

> **Just to reiterate** — this book is **NOT** about MARKETING. It is the process that, ideally, comes BEFORE the marketing efforts. Here, you will be clarifying your unique value position that you would then use to *go to market, more consciously, strategically and deliberately.*

Clarifying your brand, at this level, is the "missing piece" in the ability to create consistencies that build trust, help you discern differently toward achieving goals faster, and establish the sustainable differentiation that enables you to enjoy competitive advantage.

Let's get started!

First, take a moment to answer these questions.

1. *If you were to describe yourself to someone who is not familiar with you, what would you say?* ("I am someone who...")

2. If you were asked, *"Why should I hire (your name),"* what would you say?

3. *If you personally had a tagline, what would it be?* (Taglines are designed to provide a short, catchy benefit for those choosing to work with you.)

PAUSE, REFLECT AND ANSWER what's at the top of your mind right now. If you don't know these answers, your friends, colleagues, and clients won't either. In this process, I'll help you model your Personal Brand after your authentic self. But we must uncover "who are you?" first and foremost to establish a solid foundation that carves out your place in the world.

> *WORTH REFLECTING:* Your challenge throughout this transformational journey is twofold; to make everything about you on the outside congruent with who you are on the inside, and then leverage the heck out of it to catapult the achievement of your goals and ambitions through what you do professionally and personally.

Now that's a tall order, but it is achievable when you commit to completing the critical due diligence—so you are here now, and I'm here to guide you towards the conscious development of your Personal Brand Presence from deep within.

It is important to know why you've committed to this process; so here are some of the benefits to come.

You will...understand that building your Personal Brand is a daily

PROCESS, not a one-time EVENT. If you are a solo-preneur, an executive, or someone who simply wants to tap into your uniqueness, this program is for you. Most people in business think that once you have your logo, tagline, collateral, website, public relations, and marketing plan together that your Brand-building is good to go. NOT SO...building your Brand is a process that must be top of mind daily to truly leverage it. And it must start from within.

As a certified trainer in delivering information to audiences that gets absorbed quickly, facilitation is in my DNA—so that is why this book is written like a workshop or course. It is full of exercises, assessments, and triggers to get you thinking deeply and uniquely internal. I hope you enjoy this deep dive and realize even the incremental changes that occur throughout with your mind, behaviors, and manifestations to come.

I will re-introduce this quote that has affirmed my direction and intention to constantly expand and grow:

"Your level of success is inextricably related to your level of personal development."

Claire Zammit, PhD., Evolving Wisdom, and Feminine Power Global Community

There will be many terms and concepts throughout this book that may seem new—and strange. That is, until you delve inside and start working on your Personal Brand Presence.

Another note I want to bring to your attention is that I will be using the term "Audience" a lot in this book to refer to all the people you engage with every day—from friends, to family, to colleagues, to your customers and prospects. It is the best word I have found that covers all those areas in your life and is charged with the energy of "attention," because they are perceiving you at all levels.

Because this program is talking to solo-professionals/solopreneurs — those who own their own company and have no employees (including independent contractors and distributors)—and simply those who desire to become more of who they say they are and reach their potential, that's all of you leaders out there, I've decided to use a collective term like "Audience" to refer to all those peoples you interact with daily.

Another reason I like the term "audience" is because it implies you are there to deliver an experience. And by understanding your Personal Brand Presence, you can begin to be more conscious of the consistent experience that defines you! You may be familiar with the term Self-Actualization—I want to dig a bit deeper into the meaning of that term and the benefits of the process.

Psychologist Abraham Maslow coined this term in his work on human desire for fulfillment and our hierarchy of needs. He states, *"What a man can be, he must be." "This need we may call self-actualization...It refers to the desire for self-fulfillment, namely, to the tendency for him to become actualized in what he is potentially. This tendency might be phrased as the desire to become more and more of what one is, to become everything that one is capable of becoming."*

So, how do we know someone is *self-actualized*?
Maslow identified key characteristics of self-actualized people:

Acceptance and Realism: Self-actualized people have realistic perceptions of themselves, others, and the world around them. Rather than being fearful of things that are different or unknown, they can view things logically and rationally.

Problem-centering: Self-actualized individuals are concerned with solving problems outside of themselves, including helping others and finding solutions to problems in the external world. These people are often motivated by a sense of personal responsibility and ethics.

Spontaneity: They are spontaneous in their internal thoughts and outward behavior. While they can conform to rules and social expectations, they also tend to be open and unconventional.

Autonomy and Solitude: Self-actualized people have a need for independence and privacy. While they enjoy the company of others, these individuals need time to focus on developing their own individual potential.

Continued Freshness of Appreciation: They tend to view the world with a continual sense of appreciation, wonder, and awe. Even simple experiences continue to be a source of inspiration and pleasure.

Peak Experiences: They often have what Maslow termed peak experiences, or moments of intense joy, wonder, awe, and ecstasy. After these experiences, people feel inspired, strengthened, renewed, or transformed.

Enjoying the Journey: While self-actualized people have concrete goals, they do not see things as simply a means to an end. The journey toward achieving a goal is just as important and enjoyable as actually accomplishing the goal.

Do you see some of these characteristics in yourself?

I've adapted Maslow's terms into a quick assessment. You will find areas to leverage and areas you might want to review. Carve out 10 minutes to do this exercise now.

[See Brand Exercises Ch1/1, Page 132
- Self-Actualization Assessment.]

Self-Actualization is important because of the way we human beings are built to take in information, process it and make daily decisions. Let's dissect this idea of knowing our "WHY'...popularized by author and motivational speaker Simon Sinek.
(https://youtu.be/u4ZoJKF_VuA)

Sinek starts out his theory of "Why," by noting that everyone knows WHAT you do—or hopefully you know because you are selling it and being it, right? The "WHAT" is interpreted by your audiences' neocortex. That part of the brain, which is responsible for our rational, analytical thought, and even the language they hear to make sense of the WHAT they are buying.

Our typical approach to interacting with others is to come from the standpoint of the "WHAT" (i.e. "I need some camping gear.")—where your audiences immediately create filters of rationalization and try to find reasons not to spend their money or believe what you say by analyzing the language they hear.

But when we focus on our HOW and WHY, we begin to reach your audience's middle two sections of the brain that make up their limbic brain—which fosters feelings, like trust and loyalty, and is responsible for all human behavior and decision-making—without the capacity for language, but it becomes the driver of behavior. (i.e. "I should buy my camping gear from REI because I know they believe in supporting the great outdoors, our environment, and my experience in it, and provide quality items I can trust).

> ***WORTH REFLECTING:*** So, when your Personal Brand communicates from the inside-out approach, and starting with the "WHY," we are talking directly to the part of the limbic brain that controls behavior, emotions, trust, loyalty, and then rationalizes it after the decision-making process. So, in understanding your "WHY" and articulating it through actions and behaviors, it will position your Personal Brand differently and more emotionally in the minds of your audience and create that connection.

"People don't buy YOU because of WHAT you do, they buy the HOW & WHY you do it..."

- Simon Sinek, Author, Speaker

Remember, *"the goal is not to influence others to have what you have... but rather the goal is to sell to those who believe what you believe,"* Sinek adds.

Now it is time to take a look at where you are in alignment with who you are. Take just a few minutes now and answer the 18 questions listed to self-assess your understanding and actioning of your Personal Brand.

Please complete this assessment before reading on.

PERSONAL BRAND PRESENCE™ SELF-ASSESSMENT
To explore and determine if you are *"thinking and acting with personal brand presence,"* complete the following questions.

Answer YES or NO to the following:

Rate the accuracy of each statement:

	YES	NO
1. Have you defined your desired *personal brand representation* formally in writing?		
2. Have you assessed your *personal values* within the last twelve (12) months?		
3. Do you know what *authentically differentiates* you from your peers?		
4. Are your actions *relevant* to your values and fundamental beliefs?		
5. Have you clearly articulated in writing a *vision* of your desired future, self-actualized state?		
6. Are you confident enough to *do, say, dress, and act* as you know you are authentically?		
7. Have you defined long term *'aspirational' goals* along with an action plan to accomplish?		
8. Do you have a *personal mantra* for yourself that describes what you stand for?		
9. Do you know what your *specific skills* and *unique qualities* are that set you apart from others?		
10. Are you *consistent* in how you describe yourself to others?		
11. Do you *know* how you *are currently perceived* by others?		
12. Do you know how you *want* to be *perceived* by others?		
13. Do you solicit *feedback* regularly from others on how you are perceived?		
14. Do others *describe* you how you want to be described?		
15. Are you living your life based on *your terms and dreams*?		
16. Have you created a *plan to 'package'* yourself in a way that reflects how *you want to be perceived*?		
17. Do you have a *mentor* or personal *coach*?		
18. Are your *physical attributes* and *presence* consistent with your desired personal brand image?		
19. Do you KNOW at least *3 things* you wish to *manifest* within the next 12 months? Please list below		
a)		
b)		
c)		

Evaluating your score: (5 points for every YES answer)
75+ = Excellent Brand Presence: You are thinking/acting like your brand to reflect your desired 'way of being.'
60 – 75 = Good Brand Presence: You have the foundation to develop a Personal Elevated Brand position and 'way of being.'
< 60 = Brand Presence Opportunity: You have significant opportunity to benefit from Elevating your Personal Brand position and 'way of being.' © Brand Ascension, LLC. All rights reserved. www.BrandAscension.com

In completing this assessment tool, what are the areas you answered "NO" to and what did that stir up for you? Many of us don't take the time in our lives to ponder these very same questions and work on answering them in a distinct, and articulate way. Imagine what would change in your daily presence if you were crystal clear and answered each of these questions with a resounding YES! Well, you're in the right place, because that is what this program will help you uncover...now, let's keep this progress moving forward!

So, just "WHAT IS A PERSONAL BRAND?" It's surprisingly simple...

> *A Personal Brand is a collection of perceptions that originates in your mind and perpetuates into the minds of your "audience." It is based on emotion and defined by their experience with you, your actions, and behaviors.*

If you were looking for the word "logo," or "image" in the definition above, you won't find it. Because your Brand is not a marketing tool like a visual logo is, but rather, it IS "the WHAT" you are marketing. And the process of branding is the process of *"assigning meaning"* to a particular entity...YOU. Logos are simply a graphic symbol that *comes to represent* your Brand (if used consistently), it isn't your Brand in and of itself. Hence, you need to clarify your Brand first, so that graphic symbol, your logo, can be used to represent what you intend for it to represent (which is perceived through your actions, behaviors, communication, and overall way of being.)!

Think about all the ways we, as humans, collect information around us to categorize, process, and form the opinions we house in our brains? Now the question becomes, "What are the ways your 'audience' also uses to form a perception of your Personal Brand?" How do they take in information to form perceptions? ...Through our senses, of course!

Well then, what are the six senses? (Yes, six, as I always include INTUITION!)

As humans we are gifted with sight, taste, sound, touch, smell, and intuition. And there are lots of creative ways we can begin affirming our brand through those sensory receptors. There's more about the use of our senses to leverage your brand later in the book, when you are ready to leverage your Personal Brand Presence DNA.

Many of you may remember the concept of "GESTALT theory" from psychology. It suggests that the sum is greater than its individual parts. We can use the term GESTALT to describe our process of perception—how we interpret and assign meaning to sensory input. What it really boils down to is that your audience is affected and MOVED by the 'GESTALT of your Personal Brand Presence.'

So, now if your Personal Brand Presence is the SUM from a set of perceptions, what perception do you want to create in the minds of your AUDIENCE, and how can YOU control that perception? You will get those answers by completing this book and all the activities.

Let's illustrate how perception works...

I want you to think about your circle of friends, colleagues, and family. Write down who you know who...[fill in their name]
- Is always late? _____
- Can never decide? _____
- Is flamboyant and loud? _____
- Is confident and professional? _____
- Is a know-it-all? _____
- Is always cynical? Or a "victim"? _____
- Is always positive? _____
- Is very motivated and driven? _____
- Is highly organized and scheduled? _____
- Is always daydreaming? _____
- Is always lucky? _____

We can likely identify with knowing someone in almost every one of these categories. These categories identify some of the perceptions we build in our minds based on what we experience with that person, oftentimes in just the first few seconds of contact! This, hence, becomes their "Personal Brand Presence" in your mind, until something changes it over time. Now, which categories do you fall into? Are the category selection(s) the same as what your colleagues might say about you? Interesting to think about, isn't it?

I want to share one of the most thought-provoking quotes I have found in the Brand-building arena. I've actually paraphrased it from James Gilmore and Joseph Pine's *THE EXPERIENCE ECONOMY* book... I adapted it slightly so it would be more relevant to this context, and it reads...

"In the absence of a distinctive Personal Brand experience, YOU become the default in your customer's purchase decision."

So, in other words, without that discerning, memorable, distinctive experience from you—your audiences have really nothing else to base the value of the experience on and will probably not file it away as memorable in their mind databank! Think about your networking experiences and how often that happens to you and your perception of others that you meet. You may only truly remember one or two distinctive people from the event, right? So what was it about them that made them memorable to you?

Not everyone consistently commands the attention of their audience like Oprah Winfrey, Tony Robbins, or even Agent 007, James Bond! But you can begin flushing out the attributes that are authentically in your unique Personal Brand Presence and leverage them to be more memorable and useful to your advantage in your everyday lives. Now, let's get crystal clear on the difference between the task of MARKETING vs. the process of BRANDING.

Many solo-professionals cannot clearly distinguish the difference between the function of marketing yourself vs. the function of building out your Brand presence. But when you understand there IS a distinct difference—you will begin to think very differently about how you are able to consciously, strategically, and deliberately, elevate your Personal Brand Presence in every situation.

Imagine yourself as one of these two people in the graphic below. Take a look at how they are dressed, how they stand, their facial expressions, and imagine their demeanor and tone of voice, and their overall personality. You can feel some perceptions forming immediately within you as you observe these elements. What is your immediate collective impression of the gentleman? The woman? (Think of and name three adjectives that describe each of them from what you perceive.) How they show up to you is how they are consciously or subconsciously marketing themselves.

MARKETING

Is the process of **COMMUNICATING** OR **DISSEMINATING** your brand's **MESSAGE** (i.e., actions, behaviors, transactions, tone, vocabulary, etc.)

[EXTERNAL]

VS.

BRANDING

Is the process of identifying, defining, and aligning your brand's **MESSAGE!** (core values, style, differentiators, standards, platform & 'WHY')

[INTERNAL]

MARKETING is the PROCESS of COMMUNICATING and SPREADING the MESSAGE.

Marketing is a key part of the external Brand experience that creates perceptions on how you go about communicating your Personal Brand to the public or your audiences. For example: It is how you dress, how you gesture, your tone of voice, how you react, how you instigate conversation, eye contact (or not), your smile, your posture, sense of confidence, approachability, etc. These are all ways to communicate externally what your Brand message represents.

Remember the concept of Gestalt I mentioned earlier? It is all these little tiny nuances that your audience picks up on to create the Brand perception of you, in an instant, and continues to formulate and adjust as they spend more time with you.

So if "Marketing" is the communication of messages, then... "BRANDING" is the process of identifying, defining (assigning meaning), and then aligning to—or living out—the message.

> ***WORTH REFLECTING:*** Think of "Personal Branding" as a process of ASSIGNING MEANING to yourself, from a highly conscious, strategic, and deliberate way, so that you can begin to manage and leverage it. This process starts at the internal level of your being with a clear understanding of what you stand for—that's your unique Personal Brand Presence. It's clarity at your DNA level, consisting of your core values and personality traits, your differentiators and skill sets, as well as your whole belief system of your life standards and expectations. When your Personal Brand is clearly defined, authentic, congruent, and is emulated consistently in your actions and behaviors and matches that of your values, style, Brand promise, and platform, your Brand begins to live its potential.

"Your marketing might get your prospects in the door, but it's your Brand that keeps them coming back."

– Suzanne Tulien

So, by now, I am sure you are wondering how you can truly maximize both in how you market and present yourself through your Brand DNA? It's simple. By ensuring that you exemplify and become more congruent and authentic through your actions, behaviors, how you dress, speak, and react according to your Personal Brand Presence DNA. When this occurs, you will be able to take control of, manage, and elevate your Personal Brand!

It seems obvious that even if you have the most entertaining and powerful display of advertising on the planet, your "marketing" efforts and will NOT be trusted longterm without a solid Personal Brand

Presence foundation established at the internal level which supports how you walk your Brand talk consistently, through and through. If this does not occur, your marketing becomes perceived as just "lipstick on a pig" as the old adage goes.

Bottom line? **You have to BE your Brand.**
Think about it: **How can you BE it if you are
not CLEAR on what IT is?**

Next, we are going to realize the extrinsic value of conscious, strategic, and deliberate Personal Brand-building over time. ...An answer to the question, "Why are we spending time in this program to identify, define, and become our own Personal Brand Presence?"

Because when we become more consistent in how we show up, we are more trusted by our peers and audiences. Take a look at the value of these powerful Personal Brands...Ed Sheeran (musician) - $206 million, Taylor Swift (music artist) $360 million, Beyonce at $400 million, Judge Judy at $420 million, Dr. Phil at $440 million, Guy Kawasaki at $30 million, Michael Jordan at 1.9 billion, Ellen DeGeneres at $490 million, and a whopping $2.7 billion for Oprah Winfrey at the time of this writing! Consistency builds trust. (source: https://thestir.cafemom.com/celebrities/223866/celebrity-net-worth-2020)

Sure, you could say these are celebrities, but they couldn't have become celebrities without becoming more consistent and conscious of who they were, personally, as a Personal Brand to be trusted, relied upon, and looked up to and followed by audiences who relate to what they stand for.

Check in with your own processes and daily business activities. How much time are you really spending on Brand-building versus marketing? Take the time to actively reflect throughout the book! When you really think about the difference in function—you Market a Brand, and if you haven't created your Brand—or at least identified and defined it...***what are you really marketing?***

> ***WORTH REFLECTING:*** When a solo-preneur (and businesses with employees for that matter) go to market their Brand,

without taking the time to identify, define and align to their Brand, they end up "chasing the client" rather than "attracting the client" due to the lack of confidence and consistency that their Brand clarity would bring them. They market from a state of guessing what they believe the prospects might want, instead of declaring a clear value position they've identified, defined, and deliver on consistently and authentically.

Next, I'll give you the 30,000 ft. view of the entire identifying, defining, and aligning process in the Personal Brand Presence DNA methodology.

My goal is to make these processes as simple and results-oriented as possible and get into the hands of savvy, like-minded solo-preneurs like you! In fact, after this section (Identify, Define & Align) is completed, know that I have a series of high impact mini workshops designed to help you begin effectively implementing your new Personal Brand Presence throughout your company and personal life—if you so choose...

[*Brand Mini Workshops Link Resource: https://bit.ly/3gmT5g5*]

Now, let's get to my Personal Brand Presence methodology – refined and adapted for the solopreneur from my "Ignite Your Business Brand DNA" methodology outlined in my book, *Brand DNA; Uncover Your Organization's Genetic Code for Competitive Advantage*. Think about what you know about the concept of human "DNA" and its function in

16

the body, from biology class in high school or college...now transfer that function into your own being, and it becomes your Personal Brand Presence DNA—it is the Dimensional Nucleic Assets® of your way of being. It is unique to you. It's the genetic blueprint for the growth, development, consistency, and evolution of your Personal Brand.

The six components of the Personal Brand Presence DNA methodology DNA are:

1) CORE VALUES – these are your guiding principles that form the basis for what is important to you, and that you strive to live by at the conscious and subconscious levels.

2) BRAND STYLE – is the manner in which you present yourself, your actions and behaviors, reflecting your distinct Personality as a Brand.

3) DIFFERENTIATORS – are the key attributes that set you apart from others, from your accomplishments, to your skill sets, to your experiences—they all play an integral role in who you are now and will be in the future.

4) STANDARDS of LIVING – are the areas of performance excellence you commit to deliver in your daily life and comprise of six "buckets" or life dimensions (Financial, Spiritual/Wellbeing, Family, Relationships, Community, Professional).

5) BRAND MANTRA and **6) BRAND "WHY" statement** – these are powerful tools to help articulate your essence and commitment for your Personal Brand Presence and used to remind you to get back to who you really are when you are out of alignment.

Each of these elements when created sequentially as presented in this book can build upon each other for a robust and meaningful examination of who you are. So, let's continue your journey of discovery.

Lesson 2: The Value of Values & How They Affect Your Personal Success

In this first chapter, I am introducing you to the first of the six Personal Brand Presence elements, core values, within the DNA process. You will be working on uncovering and defining yours in a step-by- step exercise!

Take your time with the remainder of this chapter so you can build upon your core values which will ultimately impact your feelings of authenticity. The clearer you are here (you'll know when you start getting goose bumps), the more powerful the rest of this program will be for you! Remember, you are building your Personal Brand Presence building blocks to uncover your unique DNA!

But first, here is a quick example of a graduate of my Personal Brand coaching program's results of one of his core value attributes and definitions.

Working with Chevy was an amazing experience. He took everything I said to heart and transformed his way of thinking toward his Personal Brand in amazing ways. Once he became crystal clear on his authentic Personal Brand attributes the flood doors opened and his creativity took off, not to mention his drive and motivation to self-actualize his DNA through his new consulting, speaking & training company called "Conduct Your Life."

Chevy was able to flush out his core Brand values as: "I value: Integrity, Excellence, Servant Leadership, and Creating Fun." I want to highlight Servant Leadership because it truly encompasses what Chevy's Personal Brand is all about. Look at his unique definition below and notice it is not from Webster's Dictionary, but rather from his heart and soul. This exercise ignited his love of life and affirmed his purpose in what he does professionally now after a long career in the Air Force. He is now on a roll with his Conduct Your Life training company.

I value Servant Leadership: *"A leadership philosophy I espouse and by which I live, is to give priority attention to the immediate and long-term needs of the people I serve. At all times, I ask myself and others how I can help achieve their goals, inspire them, solve their problems, and promote personal development. My mindset always leans towards helpfulness as I seek to find solutions to challenges that will up-level others. This mindset keeps me humble and grateful for all I have and do. "* – Chevy C.

(I'll share more of his values definitions a bit later.)

The importance of identifying and defining what you value creates ablueprint for how you lean into and take more control in how you show up in your world, how you create on-brand experiences and perpetuate how you want to be known for by living a values-driven life. Your values are at the core of your being—whether you've noticed or not—and are part of the ingredients to build out your own unique Personal Brand Presence DNA.

Lesson 3 will take you through the depths of this concept and the activity of identifying and defining your core values.

"Until you make the unconscious conscious, it will direct your life and you will call it fate."

-Carl Jung, Swiss Psychiatrist & Psychoanalyst-

Lesson 3: Identifying & Defining Your Personal Brand Values

This delineation could be the hardest part of the process. But realize that at your core, there are very few attributes that are fundamental to who you are. However, these attributes can show up at so many levels —when they are the right ones—and you will be able to see and feel how they expand to include the whole essence of you.

In this lesson, you will be focusing on developing or refining your own core values through your first official exercise. The only way we can truly live out our values is if we identify and define them, so that we can become conscious of them.

WHAT ARE VALUES?

I define Values as those "Guiding Principles" that reflect your core ideology. They are essential to everything you do within your professional and personal life. They underpin your decision-making process and your actions, and create the filters for your experiences. These carefully crafted and chosen attributes reflect the core of who you are, authentically, right now, not what you want to aspire to become.

But first, in a video interview of my client, attorney Brenda Speer, she showcases how she is leveraging some unusual Brand attributes and core values every day in her law practice. She is carving out her distinction by infusing her authenticity into her profession.

Let's watch this client interview: ***https://youtu.be/XAFZiQaXdRc***

Does this video make you think of how your Personal Brand may or may not be living through your own core values?

Would uncovering or revealing your authentic attributes make you nervous if your core values were seemingly different from those of others in your same field of expertise?

Our values are under attack every day of our lives by all the external forces we are exposed to regularly. When we identify and define our own values, it is like adding "insulation" to our well-being and helping us to become more and more internally driven vs. externally impacted.

Think about it: Building a Brand that aligns with who you are can be challenging and it can make you push outside of your current comfort zone. A Personal Brand that is truly you might not look exactly like what others in your field would expect. And you may realize that you have not yet really begun to express your values within your professional environment, or even within your personal relationships. These are the "aha" moments that can be expected when doing this deeper work on ourselves. Note that many of us have values that have been ignored, trapped, or kept on the down-low for many reasons. Now is the time to get clarity on what those are, feel the authentic release and liberation of acknowledging them, and start living them fully.

Does your Personal Brand defy some of the stereotypes of your profession in the way that Attorney Brenda Speer's did in the video? Are you prepared to make your Brand an honest representation of who you are? It could be the most freeing feeling you can have. Trust in the process. At the end of this chapter, I will take you through two steps to get you through this process.

But before you dive into action with the exercise... let's take a moment to hone in on what we mean by "defining your core values" with some more client examples.

Here, again, is my client, Chevy and his list and definitions that come from the position of how his Personal Brand lives out the values within his everyday life.

"I value…

INTEGRITY: At all times I represent the truth; keep my commitments and promises; I adhere to our firm's standards and ethics; accurately represent my competencies; and always act in the best interests of the client and the firm. I have and consciously create honest, transparent relationships and seek out others who want the same. I am honest with myself and reflect often on my actions and behaviors to ensure my alignment. I aim to offer my best self, consistently.

EXCELLENCE: I insist on excellence in all products and services; I make quality service a top priority; I constantly strive for innovation and improvement; and continually contribute to developments in the field of leadership training. Being excellent is being in my alignment. I am constantly growing and learning to continue expansion and become a better cocreator with those I connect with. Excellence in my way of being is a state of mind.

SERVANT LEADERSHIP: The leadership philosophy I espouse and by which I live, is to give priority attention to the immediate and long-term needs of the people I serve. At all times, I ask how I can help others to achieve their goals, solve their problems, and promote personal development. My mindset always leans towards helpfulness as I seek to find solutions to challenges that will up-level others. This mindset keeps me humble and grateful for all I have and do.

CREATE FUN: While I take leadership training seriously, I inject fun (including music!) into my programs because I know how laughter opens the creative mind to learning and that music makes it memorable. I seek out the joy in all situations. I love to make others laugh and see humor and humility within myself. I believe creating fun empowers me and others to become more innovative and attract more positivity in our experiences. I thrive in organizing social events, hosting dinner parties, and designing fun into all my situations.

The key point here is that customizing your value definitions grounds the meaning and makes it crystal clear as to the expectation of the value and how it is actioned within your life, every day, person to person. Remember, these definitions showcase the "HOW" your brand delivers on the value in every facet of your world.

Meet Melissa, a nationally certified wellness coach, and Personal Brand graduate client, through her Brand Values:

"I value...

CONFIDENCE: I affirm my accomplishments and successes, and those of my clients. I acknowledge where confidence in one area can positively impact and support increasing confidence in other areas. I lean into others who are strong and confident about who they are and like to surround myself around those who naturally see the possibilities of their own expansion.

CONNECTEDNESS: I connect to myself, to family/friends, to clients, and to community through my experience, interests, and profound curiosity. I rely on my desire and commitment to connection most profoundly when experiencing the disconnect that comes when faced with conflict, differing perspectives or belief systems, and when feeling most alone.

COURAGE: I regularly step outside my comfort zone and the limitations set by myself and others. I seek out and provide guidance when fear rears its ugly head and threatens to derail efforts in overcoming challenges, adversity, and the desire to grow. I support others to step outside their comfort zone in the desire to draw on courage in expanding what is possible in their lives.

PROGRESS: I have a sense of the future always being more than the now. When the tangible outcomes my clients or my desire is not fully reached, I encourage the acknowledgement of progress and the promise of possibility. No accomplishment is insignificant when moving in the direction of overcoming challenges, stepping outside one's comfort zone, and moving towards the best version of self.

You can really begin to "know" her just by reading her value definitions. So, what if you don't go to this detail? What are the implications of not clarifying your values and not living up to those values?

It can mean complete annihilation of business and severely tarnished personal images. It takes years and a lot of work to earn the trust back of your friends, colleagues, and customers when you've lost it. Not to mention the possibility of never reaching your full potential because you're stuck.

I had a client in the travel industry who was super sharp, highly independent, an adventurer, planner, and skilled at so many entrepreneurial tasks. However, she was spinning her wheels and getting very little traction on her business growth goals. She realized she was chasing too many things in order for her to show up doing what she thought her clients wanted. When she completed this personal brand clarity work, she shifted to becoming more internally driven, confident in her brand style, she started doing what she loves, specifically, in her business (international adventure travel), and started attracting all sorts of new clients and opportunities to grow exponentially.

Defining your values with specificity enables you to have greater control over the impact they have in your life. Clarity is the basis for action.

Again, it's important that your personal values not just be words on paper, but actioned and lived in every facet of your life and business. Great Personal Brands keep their core values at the forefront of their decision-making, their behaviors, and how they inspire, engage, recognize, and treat their customers, vendors, friends, and family. Their values even impact how they package and deliver their products and run their business.

Perception truly is everything. Holding true to and living up to your values will only enhance the impression and consistency perceptions of your Personal Brand Presence.

As I promised in the intro—I'll now share with you a few of my core values and my own unique definitions to further exemplify the depth of meaning they provide to me and how they ground me in being who I know and say I am. Here are two of them…

"I value…

CONSCIOUSNESS: I pride myself on being visually, emotionally, and energetically aware of the people, situation, and energy around me. I "read" my audiences with care and respect and respond appropriately to ensure the best possible experience. I value respect, and notice others who are highly emotionally intelligent. I lean into deeper, intellectual discussions about life and the human element. I love being in expansion mode vs. contraction, so I regularly seek cutting edge information and innovations that help increase my level of knowing more about the fascinating workings of our universe and those experiencing it.

TRANSPARENCY: What you see is what you get with me. I am driven to be authentic in my approach to life, in what I say, and with my audiences. I seek the truth, equality, and clarity in every situation so that I can respond with the same. I follow my gut and it often inspires me, and I lean into those who express theirs with curiosity. By consciously creating an "accepting" environment, I cocreate the drawing out of more transparency in others to enhance the overall human experience between myself and my audiences. Transparency to me is grounded in TRUTH.

In order to write these definitions for my values, I had to sit still, put my "transparency" shoes on and think about how I show up in that space. Then, the words start to come with ease and flow. You can do the same. This is the work.

When thinking about identifying and defining your Personal Brand Values, the next question is "how and where can you implement these values in your everyday personal and business environment?" You see, your values don't just surface in professional settings, they should be part of your DNA and infused into how you "show up" in every facet of your life.

WORTH REFLECTING: The ultimate power of your chosen values is the ability to express it in every detail and act that you personally and your company perform. By their very nature the combination of these attributes creates distinction like no other. And these values added to the rest of your defined Brand DNA carves out an even more unique experience for you to express in your way of being.

Here are some areas to begin implementing and leveraging your new Brand values into areas of your life such as:

WORK LIFE:

- Strategic goals and objectives can be designed to perpetuate and align to your values.
- Performance Reviews/Metrics – are you living up to your values?
- Marketing/Promotions – your messages can reveal to your customers what you truly value and align to their core values to create a deeper level of connection.
- Communications to Customers, Vendors, and Your Community – speaking with your values at the forefront of your intention supports your tone and how others receive you.
- Follow-up communications.
- Onboarding clients and serving them.
- Acquiring & firing clients.
- Partnering with vendors.
- Work/life balance.

PERSONAL LIFE:

- Relationships/Love – like-hearted people create deeper levels of coherence and sustain longer, more meaningful relationships
- Family environment – family core values are the glue for communications, trust, and joy.
- Life decisions/Financial/Wellness – your core values can guide you to discern differently, and affirm your choices.

- Career aspirations – knowing your values can lead you in amazing directions that align your being to your passions.
- Behaviors.
- Choosing friendships.
- Releasing friendships.
- Creating an environment that enables your values to be lived.

I hope this list has spurred some ideas in your mind as to the "value of values" and where to begin applying them within your business and personal life as soon as you can. It is a consciousness that you are now enabled to have because of your clarity of what your values are. Now that I've covered values from my Personal Brand Presence DNA model, let's move onto the next core DNA attribute to develop.

Congratulations! You are now on the road to creating a powerfully solid infrastructure for your Personal Brand elevation! Utilize the work and knowledge you gleaned from this chapter to start thinking about how you will implement your Personal Brand Presence DNA attributes through all the facets of your business! Collaborate with others who care about your well-being and success, who believe in your business Brand, and will provide you with a trusted sounding board and feedback on your exercise outputs.

> ***WORTH REFLECTING:*** Take note and be cautious of what I call "the peanut gallery" (your audiences)! If done correctly and with focused intention, your outputs of these exercises should resonate deeply with you. When you reach out and ask others you trust for feedback, listen with discernment and weigh what they tell you with what you know to be true. Reflect and assess whether their feedback gets implemented or you just realize the gap between who you know you are and what others have been experiencing of you. Ahh, now, that is something to ponder!

Before we move into the next chapter, let's review some key areas of what we learned in your Personal Brand Presence Chapter 1 and finally carve out the time to take action on the exercises.

LET'S RECAP! Take a moment and see if you can answer each of these review questions to see what you remember! I hope these were easy for you.

Here are the answers...

- **WHAT IS A Personal Brand?** Your Personal Brand is just a set of overall perceptions others have of you—ideally, it starts within your own heart and mind (and is expressed through your actions and behaviors).
- **WHAT IS THE DIFFERENCE BETWEEN MARKETING VS BRAND-BUILDING?** Marketing is the process of communicating your Personal Brand's message (in a variety of platforms) vs. Brand-building which is the process of identifying, defining, and aligning (or living) your Personal Brand's message.
- AND, finally, most of us know WHAT it is we do every day, but rarely do we really take the time to identify and define the "WHY" we do it. Remember, people don't buy your WHAT, they buy your "WHY!" (Simon Sinek)
- Your Personal Brand values are your guiding principles that help you discern situations and challenges throughout your life and align to your authentic self.

Schedule time to work on and complete the remaining Chapter 1 exercises now:

Step One: Identify Your Personal Brand Values -
See Brand Exercise Ch1/2, Page 133

I take you through a series of thought-provoking questions that when answered will enable you to uncover your core values. And if you already have a set of values, I highly encourage you to go through and answer the questions in the prepared exercise as it will either validate or uncover something that is missing.

Step Two: Define Your Personal Brand Values -
See Brand Exercise Ch1/3, Page 136

Why should you define your values? Well, terms can have different meanings for different people. Get specific in how you define your values because they are unique in their meaning to you (connotative) and should not be defined via the Webster dictionary (denotative). Don't go to the dictionary, you already know these words you chose, but rather really think through what they mean to you and HOW you show up in your actions and behaviors living these values and come up with your own composition for each.

You have step-by-step instructions within the exercises. Make sure you study the examples to provide you a clear direction and some inspiration on this exercise. I also want to encourage you to carve

out enough time to really dig into this exercise. After the full review of this chapter, you deserve the time you are giving this and will reap the benefits of this effort in the near future!

Have fun with this and make it a big deal when you complete it by celebrating it.

Remember, this is all about uncovering what makes you, YOU! Commit now to staying focused and get elevated!

"Your marketing might
get your prospects
in the door, but it's your
Personal Brand
that keeps them
coming back."

– Suzanne Tulien,
Brand Clarity Expert,
Brand Ascension

CHAPTER 2

YOU'VE GOT STYLE, BUT ARE YOU LEVERAGING IT?

If you have completed Chapter 1, activities and all, then you are ready to dive into Chapter 2, Define your Personal Brand Style! This next chapter is a continuation of your deep dive into you, specifically identifying your unique personality and "way of being!"

Yes, you do have style! Everyone does! We are like snowflakes, each one of us is uniquely different from each other. The goal in this work is to uncover your core Personal Brand Style Attributes and begin to leverage them in how you go about delivering on your Personal Brand. This is about taking "ownership" of who you are and how you go about being more you, more "on-brand," daily.

Upon Completion of Chapter 2, you will be able to:

1. IDENTIFY your Personal Brand's unique Style Attributes.
2. DEFINE your Personal Brand's unique Style Attributes.
3. LEARN where and how to implement your Brand's Style Attributes into your personal and professional life to create consistency and real distinction.

Once you uncover your set of key style (personality) attributes, you can begin designing and shaping customer touch points throughout your business and get more conscious about how you approach and solve daily challenges, build relationships, and create a more stylish, aligned environment for yourself.

Knowing your Brand Style will also contribute greatly to designing your customer's experience so that they get to know you better and begin to trust who you are and build deeper connections.

Your Personal Brand Style can help hone your marketing messaging, it's tone and pace...and will also be used and infused into your actions and behaviors at a much more conscious level, enabling you to live authentically and thrive.

I am excited for you to unpack what makes you, you in this fun and a bit more creative chapter. Think of this as an exercise in self-authoring your life! Here you become more internally driven, instead of externally impacted by your situations and environment.

So, remember to carve out quality time in your calendar for yourself as you are committing to creating a powerful Personal Brand foundation for living your full potential through consistency and distinction.

I invite you to get creative and have some fun with this process! And explore a little bit more and see what comes to the surface in the next chapter. This next activity challenges your creative side by getting you to use the right side of your brain.

Lesson 1: What Is Your Personal Brand's Style?

What is your Personal Brand's Style? As you develop an answer uniquely yours, you will notice how your Personal Brand showcases itself so you can consciously and deliberately step into it and start to name and give meaning to what makes you, you.

"You are not your thoughts; you are the OBSERVER of your thoughts."

- Amit Ray

Now, we are moving into the next dimension of your Personal Brand Presence DNA.

In this section, I want you to think of owning a word in the minds of your audiences. What ONE word would you choose to own that would describe your current Brand's Style?

Take a moment to think about your overall personality and the experience others have of you as they do business with you or they network with you or they are just interacting with you. You and your energy. Can you write down a descriptive adjective that represents your Brand Style overall that captures your essence, default vibration? Try jotting down the first word that may come to your mind.

This may not be as easy as you think. Because you are looking for something that is all-encompassing, right? And that is hard, but don't worry about all the varieties of possibilities, just jot down the adjective that comes to mind first and foremost about YOU—right now... _____.

Now that you've written down your word, ask yourself this:

- Would your friends use the same or similar word?
- Would your customers say the same or similar word?
- And would your family say the same or similar word?

One of the great benefits of consciously crafting your unique DNA is that you will be able to create consistency in how you want others to perceive you. You'll generate trust and loyalty longterm and build a solid Brand perception through a plethora of experiences.

This question was designed to get you into a strategic mindset thinking about how you perceive your own Brand and how others may perceive it. And to also get you thinking about how you might secure this perception consistently.

> **Note:** Choosing one word is not easy and might get you thinking in a whirlwind. It's like picking ONE tattoo to have permanently drawn on your body—what would that represent? Most of us would take the time to really think this through so that the word we choose is all-encompassing of our essence. I asked you to think about this to get your attention and begin to wonder what that word would be. However, rest assured, your Personal Brand Style will be made up of a set of words that have deep meaning, resonate with you, and underpin the foundational aspects of your unique way of being. So, take a breath, relax—this exercise will be creative and fun.

Identify Distinct Personal Styles

Three celebrity Personal Brands that have very distinct styles are:

> **Elon Musk** (CEO of Tesla)
> ***Entrepreneurial Mindset***: tenacious, strategic, risk-taker
>
> **Lady Gaga** (Singer, Actress)
> ***Consistently Inconsistent:*** creative, expressive, confident
>
> **Stephen Colbert** (Comedian/Talk Show Host)
> ***Insightful***: intellectual, satirical, mischievous

This is a good exercise to get a sense of how powerfully consistent these Brands have been and are showing up representing what their personality is to their audience.

The Brands that are the most memorable are ones that consistently create and live up to that unique style that you know them for.

Your Personal Brand Style evolves from your default way-of-being. It will be a small collection of key terms that will come together to truly capture who you are in how you show up at your default.

Why default? All of us can get out of alignment now and then. And it is recognizing your default way of being that brings you back to your power center and realigns you to who you really are. Flushing out these key terms in this exercise is powerfully transformational.

One last example of a powerfully aligned Personal Brand Style is, guess who? Oprah Winfrey! She is well-known worldwide with a style that is in everything she says, does, and represents. She is well-aware of her style attributes and lives them daily.

OPRAH IS...
Thoughtful, Curious, Genuine, Warm, Generous

OPRAH IS NOT...
Frivolous , Deceitful, Stingy, Cold/Closed

When you focus on your unique personality you will also be able to leverage those personality traits in highly consistent and relevant ways within your own industry as well as with your family, friends, colleagues, and your community. Remember, clarity is the basis for action!

What is your Personal Brand Style?

...Your basic manner/approach in which you present and deliver consistent actions and behaviors over a variety of everyday situations.

It is the personality you consistently become known for and a big contributor for designing a unique, memorable Personal Brand experience.

So, Lady Gaga has set a standard now of how people expect her to behave and visually show up. She is creative, highly self-expressive and bold in her approach, and making statements based on her beliefs and worldview. Her creativity keeps people guessing as to what she will create and even look like next. A type of Personal Brand that is surprisingly unpredictable. She has created a huge following because of her consistency in showing up in a very distinct way; *consistently inconsistent.*

This example isn't to say that you need to be as bold as Lady Gaga. What it is saying is that creating distinction can happen in a variety of ways. One of the most powerful ways is in your consistency in applying your Personal Brand Style attributes.

Questions will start arising in you, like, "How do I package my Personal Brand Style and into an experience for my professional and my personal life? What does it look like through my dress, my behaviors, and my actions?"

Other questions, like, "How do I spend my personal time and does it fit with my overall Personal Brand Presence? Does it fit with who I say I am? How do I express it in my dress?" This may sound a bit odd but if your dress in your personal time is not in sync with your style, then you need to look at why that is—and if necessary, align to it.

Think also about your spirituality/faith and what sorts of causes; (environmental, non-violence, homeless, medical issues, foster children, etc.) you may be interested in. Do they fit your personality style? How are you consciously relating to these causes; how can this feed your soul more?

Keeping tabs on your health and wellness, what do you do for yourself? How does it manifest in your style? Are you passionate about feeling good, physical fitness, nutrition? If so, where does that belief show up in your world?

As you continue to process through your entire Personal Brand Presence DNA, you will begin shaping your internal environment to build the exact perceptions you want your audience to perceive about you. The more authentic you are with these outputs, the easier it is for others to "receive" those perceptions from you. It takes time to identify and define them, so you have the construct to make it tangible and stay in your lane so you're not all over the board with your marketing (communication of your Brand). This process helps refine and align you to who you say you are and creates a construct that you can build experiences, narrative, and services around it.

Schedule about 30—45 minutes and rev up your brain power for the completion of this creative exercise.

You will be identifying and selecting your style attributes (adjectives), following a series of creative questions that will force you to think and feel about things you resonate with, that when answered will bring you to a level of authenticity and help you uncover those key terms that reflect your core style attributes.

It is important to be honest and trust your first instinct – and to allow yourself to FEEL what it is you resonate with and why. Keep checking in with yourself throughout this process as reflection is one of our best abilities to center, realign, and become more aware.

LET'S RECAP!
- What ingredients make up your Personal Brand's Style?
- Think about how you want your Brand to be perceived by your "audiences." Ensuring that it actually is authentic to you. Remember, you are not aspiring to be anything but more of your true self.
- Are you regularly expressing yourself in congruence to those perceptions consistently?

Time to dig in and uncover your Personal Brand Style. Are you ready to shift into the right side of your brain?

[See Brand Exercise Ch2/1 Page 138
– Identify Your Personal Brand Style.]

Lesson 2: Getting More Consistent & Distinctive in Leveraging Your Own Style

Now that you have identified your core set of Personal Brand Style attributes, it is time to provide detail in how you live them. By doing so, you are on the path of enabling a deeper level of awareness of who you are, which leads to consistencies in your actions and behaviors that build trust with your audiences.

"How you are ONE way is how you are Every Way."

– T. Harv Eker, Author of Bestseller, *Secrets of the Millionaire Mind*

Eker used this quote often in his workshops and trainings when it came to changing your money habits. He was often posed the question about how people change when they come into a lot of money. And his response was no, not really. If you are, at your core, a generous person, then you will be even more generous if you came into a lot of money. If you are, at the core, a greedy person, then you will be even more greedy if you came into a lot of money.

His quote above reminds us that we cannot be consistently inauthentic. In other words, we cannot be who we are not for an extended period. Our true self always surfaces in one way or another and is our default at the core. If we have a personality trait that is, say "adventurous," then we will approach life as an adventure, take risks, seek out new situations, explore more, etc. Makes sense, right? So what T. Harv Eker means in this quote is that no matter what situation we are in, there is a core set of default characteristics that we have that defines our responses to our external environments and situation. It is in our DNA, we cannot deny it.

Many of us think we have to be someone different at work than we are at home or with friends. As much as you try to be different, you cannot sustain it. It just adds more stress to your heart/mind/body and keeps you out of alignment. Once we are able to clarify and "name" our attributes, we give meaning to them, embrace them, and understand how we can go about expressing them in every facet of our world while staying in alignment with who we are.

The point of this is to truly understand and leverage your authentic self in every way possible by identifying and defining your Personal Brand Style attributes. Then, consciously notice when you are in alignment and start deliberately caring enough about how that *feels* to actively bring yourself back into it when you unconsciously weave out of your own "alignment lane."

This exercise invites and guides you to use the right side of your brain, which is the creative side, to imagine correlations your personality has to specific items. It will force you to connect your emotions toward representative objects (this is the right-brain part) and uncover where your personality leans into a perception you have of these items. Use your imagination, reflect, and tap into your creativity to resonate powerfully with this unique exercise.

You will see why it is you are drawn to these items you choose and hopefully spur a wonder as to why you might currently not be surrounded by these same things. If they represent your brand, how come they are not in your everyday experience? Food for thought!

"In order to MANAGE a PERCEPTION, we have to formulate a CONCEPTION."

-Suzanne Tulien

Define your Personal Brand Style Attributes.

Your 4—5 final adjectives from the "Identify Personal Brand Style Attributes" exercise in this chapter sets you up to create a unique definition of each term (just like you did for your Brand Values). This will deepen and solidify the meaning of your selected Personal Brand Style words *(See example sets of Personal Brand Style attribute definitions at the end of this chapter for guidance.)*

Your personal definitions for your set of Style attributes should explain *how you show up and live out* each attribute. Think about each area of your life; how each attribute you are defining shows up within your family environment, your professional environment, your community, is reflected in how you think about your financial health and overall body, mind, and spiritual wellness. Reflecting on these different facets of your life will help you flush out how you perpetuate this attribute in your way of being. Your specificity in your compositions of your definitions will enable these attributes to become more and more tangible to you.

Spending quality time on this defining practice is transformational for my clients and will kickstart your creativity in implementing your Personal Brand Presence DNA when you complete the process.

"In the absence of a distinctive Personal Brand experience, YOU become a commodity in the minds of your customers, colleagues, family, and friends."

- Paraphrased from James Gilmore and Joseph Pine, The Experience Economy

---

Your Brand style, when clearly defined, becomes a powerful tool for you to show up consistently, begin to carve out distinction, and to create memorable experiences. Remember the Pygmalion Effect, or self-fulfilling prophecy? When you become more aware of who you are, you start living it more.

How do you make your Personal Brand Style tangible?

Areas You Can Consider Infusing Your Brand Style Attributes: When you have your definitions completed, consider the following list of areas you can begin to infuse your Brand Style into your environment. Let the creative process begin!

Personal Physical Space & Office Environment

What does your space/residence/work place look like? Contemporary, Corporate, Traditional, Playful, Fun, Relaxing, Innovative? It should reflect who you are. When you start consciously designing your space with your Brand Style (and Values) in mind, you subconsciously align to it in so many ways.

For example, if the word "inspirational" flushed out as one of your Brand Style words, then you might want to get inspirational posters or images with quotes framed and hung on your walls.

I often ask my clients about their office environment, and if it currently is the color chosen in their Brand Style activity. Most of them realize they don't have the color they said represented themselves from the activity anywhere within their view. And guess what, they also don't have a lot of clothes in their wardrobe with that color! Why not? If this is the color that would represent you, why aren't you surrounded by it more often? Something to ponder!

Delivery of Your Products & Services

Your Brand style should be infused into your overall approach to serving your clients. How can you redesign your initial contact meeting to reflect your style? What elements can you add to your service delivery that showcases one or more of your style attributes to give the customer a certainty about what your Personal Brand represents? What about your process of following up or even nurturing your client base - how can you add your style through actions and behaviors, or narrative in your messaging to make it 'tangible' in the minds of your market?

Communication/Marketing (*ALL WRITTEN COMMUNICATION, ADS, PR/NEWS, Brand SPEAK, "VOICE," TONE, MARKETING CHANNELS, ETC.*)

It all needs to match - meaning be visually and tonally the same, consistent, congruent. I see so many solopreneurs whose "look and feel" are all over the spectrum! Their business cards and brochures look different than their websites, creating lots of incongruencies and therefore loose trust.

Think about this, if your Style is about fun and humor, then ensure your communications relay that to all who encounter you. Make your content a little lighter, a bit airy and positive. This showcases you and affirms you as you want to be seen and gets the attention of those prospects who appreciate and lean into that Brand Style! i.e. the more you represent your authentic self, the more you begin to attract the clients who are a perfect fit to working with you! (Take a moment to ponder that!)

My CPA firm has a very fun tone to their email communications. It makes them feel like they are human, as they make fun of all the headaches that tax season brings us all. Their tone is personable, light, and funny while trying to educate their clients on what needs they are doing to support them. It really gives you a great sense of who they are and how they manage their staff and clients.

41

Visual Identity/Logo (COLOR, FONT, GRAPHIC, TAGLINE, ETC.) Remember, your logo is NOT YOUR BRAND but rather a symbol that represents your brand. So make sure you are consistent with your Brand's chosen identity/logo colors, fonts, and overall environment. Don't use any fonts or colors that aren't visually aligned with your logo. It will feel incongruent. Make sure you use those same fonts in your marketing materials, even your emails if possible. What does your email signature look like? Is it "on-Brand" or not so much? Don't manipulate your logo graphic in any way on anything you use to represent your business (i.e. stretch it out of proportion to fit a certain space or change color for the fun of it). Your logo should stay consistent to enable it to do its job of representing your Brand and building trust through visual consistency.

Protect the integrity of the graphic symbol that represents you! If you can, consider putting together a "graphic standards" manual or a one-pager that defines how your logo should be used appropriately. It includes all the specifications of font, colors, tagline usage, etc. This can be sent to vendors when you are purchasing any items like logoed coffee mugs, phone cases, or water bottles in order to ensure the vendor does not manipulate your visual identity!

Your Website

If your Personal Brand Style is "warm and friendly," you will need to ensure that your website comes across as that to your audience as they navigate through it. This means warmer colors, lots of pictures depicting friendliness, etc. Your content or narrative has to be written with that warm tone as wells. Same goes if you have the Personal Brand Style of 'FUN' and "VIVACIOUS"—your site look and feel should reflect that— bright colors, action images, and content that reads with lots of energy and inspiration.

WORTH REFLECTING: Where can you be more consistent? I have an exercise for you in Chapter 6 to assess your consistency. But for now, start noticing and matching how your environment is showing up through your key Personal Brand Style Attributes. This is an exercise in getting highly conscious of how you are representing yourself. Creating cognitive resonance for your audience to perceive is key to establishing a Brand value position, or distinction in their minds.

Now, below are two sets of Brand Style definitions written by my clients. You can see how Personal these definitions are to them (and no one else). They dug deep and reflected on how they show up in life with each of these attributes they've chosen to best reflect who they are.

Brand Style Definition Example #1 is from a Personal Brand Presence graduate who is a real estate agent: Meet Teresa, through her Brand Style attributes...

I AM:

A GUARDIAN: I protect and care for the interests of my clients, family & friends and defend them from those who would intentionally or unintentionally take advantage. I believe in equanimity and find solutions that protect and support both sides. I seek harmony in my life situations and contribute to the security of my and others' well-being.

PERSISTENT: Despite difficulty or opposition, I tenaciously stay the course. I am good at adjusting and looking for ways to move toward goals; I like to help others stay on track. I am always looking for ways to find winning solutions. My drive for clarity and growth keeps me on task to finish what I've started and continue my momentum towards my ultimate growth. I appreciate the start of new projects and enjoy celebrating milestones of accomplishment—it gives me a sense of meaning and lots of joy to unleash my abilities.

GRACIOUS: I am compassionate and kind, always courteous, respectful, and dignified to myself and others. I know I have the power to co-create better experiences and use that power through my attention to be more gracious in my approach to living my life. I see evidence of positive outcomes regularly and bring hope and truth to others I connect with.

COMPASSIONATE: I have deep sympathy and empathy for the struggles my friends, colleagues, and family faces, and have a strong desire to actively pursue alleviating their suffering, by finding solutions that meet their goals. I consider others' situations, beliefs, and worldviews and strive to better understand them so I can support them in unique ways to live their best lives.

ENTHUSIASTIC: I am intense, passionate, and dedicated to finding positive solutions for every difficulty I and those around me may face and seek out and recognize the "silver lining" in everyone's unique journey. I have an ability to see the silver lining in even the most challenging of scenarios and practice holding the space of positivity in moving into joy as much as possible.

And Brand Style Definition Example#2, Phoenix is an adventure Travel Agent :

I AM:

SELF-AWARE: I have a clear perception of myself and am mindful of my physical and emotional existence. I am aware of and make conscious while observing thoughts and feelings as they occur in myself and in others. I easily become adaptable to the energy level, location, and environment around me. This balance helps me understand my clients, stay focused, and when necessary adapt to the current situation.

ADVENTUROUS: I am an adventurer. I am driven to explore and discover new places, things, and ideas. I crave new, multi-sensory experiences. This bold part of my Personality enables me to be the risk taker for my clients, leading the way first so they can experience through me. I learn and grow through my curiosity, and it inspires me to evolve and fulfills my quest for more in life.

INQUISITIVE: I am genuinely curious about the world and the people in it. I thrive on exploring and discovering new places, cultures, history and more. I want to KNOW about life, love, experiences, and learning new things. I learn through asking lots of questions and getting answers inspires me to move forward, take the next steps, and be an encouragement to my friends and family!

RESOURCEFUL: I am resourceful and creative in how I find out the answers to things. With my educational background, business mindset, and adventurous spirit, I find that I am capable of solving problems, finding answers, and can predict outcomes with ease. Others experience me as proactive instead of reactive in how I conduct myself personally and professionally. I am confident, I can find answers to most every question and situation.

PLAYFUL: I am playful because it helps me stay realistic and relaxed. I am consciously generating ways to be more playful in every aspect of my life. I help lighten the load of stressful situations. Life is an adventure, one of mystery and excitement. I love helping my clients, friends, and family find the joy in life again by getting out of their zip code and exploring the world to find themselves!

So how can you actualize and continue to be more and more of you? If you don't know who you are, or what your Brand is, it's a little difficult, yes? Your Brand DNA is the engine that fuels your inspiration and motivation. To stay consistent and heighten your confidence levels to be more of who you really are while uniquely serving your perfect client. It helps you stay in the lane of being you.

Ask those who know you well to confirm the attributes you decided on and to help you see how you are perceived by others.

CAUTION: Don't be too swayed if they suggest other ways that your style attributes are seen. Because it might just mean that you haven't fully leveraged who you are and how you align with your named attributes. And, you might be showing up out of alignment to appease your environment—it takes practice to get out of those habits! Believe me, we all do it. But once you are clearer and begin consciously living within your own Personal Brand Presence, you will resist weaving out of your "lane" and feel more confident to stay in your lane and represent your authentic self.

Trust what comes out of this activity for yourself and contemplate the resonance of your attribute words. You're reaching for the goose bump factor!

The secret ingredient of running a successful business is You. By going through this book and really digging into your Personal Brand—that is, taking control of how you authentically show up to create a unique experience, you are unlocking your full potential. Knowing and owning your core Values and Style will help you become known as a values-centered business.

The clarity will aid you in becoming highly discerning about who you choose to work with and how you manage your growth. And uncovering and understanding your unique Brand Style Attributes and keeping them top of mind when you consider how you go about marketing and delivering on your Brand promise, is what truly creates competitive advantage and memorable experiences that inspire your customers to become advocates.

So, identifying, defining, and aligning to your unique Personal Brand is what will distinguish you from your competition. Your competitors can copy your products and pricing all day long. They can even mimic your look and feel. But what they cannot do is be YOU in their delivery of service experience.

> **WORTH REFLECTING:** *Remember, no Brand is universal in their appeal to everyone. And the moment you realize that, is the moment you are liberated to become more of YOU.*

You are unique and leveraging your value position is key to sustainability. Building a powerful audience/customer base and staying in your own lane will strengthen your position in the market.

Start noticing how your Personal Brand clarity impacts so much more than your professional life. The clearer you get about who you are means the more impact you have on the designing of all the areas of your life.

It will be fun to start realizing how your level of Personal Brand consciousness and gradual alignment impacts your environment and your ability to manifest more of what you want and is congruent to who you are.

LET'S RECAP!
- What distinctive Personal "[Style" is your primary default?
- Are you hesitant to be distinct because it defies the "norm" in your industry or circle of friends?
- Are you being congruent to your own level of distinction?
- Are you ready to not only identify, but define your key style attributes so you can begin to consciously infusing them into your everyday life?

It's time to take action and DEFINE each Personal Brand Presence Style Attribute you uncovered in the previous exercise. This is the most important part of making your style more tangible in your actions and behaviors.

I can't wait for you to realize the power of your Personal Brand Style!

[See Brand Exercise Ch2/2, Page 141
-Define Your Brand Style.]

"Personal Brand alignment is the catalyst for your on-brand manifestations."

— Suzanne Tulien,
Brand Clarity Expert,
Brand Ascension

———

CHAPTER 3

YOU ARE YOUR OWN COMPETITIVE ADVANTAGE

Wow! This is a lot of work, isn't it? Maybe even a labor of love? But remember, most entrepreneurs don't take the time to do this important Brand foundational work, which is why the statistic reported by Forbes magazine that states "50% of startups fail within the first 5 years" is so powerful.

But I know you're here to be a part of the 50% who succeed by continuing to expand!

Even though your value and style attributes create a powerful level of distinction with your Personal Brand, this is more to do in this section that will take you on an even deeper dive into all the unique things you have done, are doing and being right now, that make you different from your competitors and colleagues! This is where we get into the quantifying of your differentiators in ways you may never have thought of. I'll show you examples later in the chapter.

Remember, no Brand is universal, not even yours. The art of finding your audience lies in your ability to get clear on what your Personal Brand is all about and how consistently you deliver on your promise! Note: When it comes to your prospects, a confused mind doesn't buy! So clarity is a fundamental strategy to increase attraction, advocacy, followers, and sales.

Regarding assessing your competitive advantage and creating distinction in your market, I want you to get into the mindset of focusing your attention only on those prospects who are already "in the market" for what you offer. In other words, they are ready to buy what you have...(from YOU or your competition). Then, think of the specific nuances you bring with what you offer, these can be small things like offering a unique guarantee or return policy, to bigger things like sought-after industry awards, higher levels of expertise and certifications, and such. Your differentiators coupled with your Values and Brand Style helps others to better understand the Gestalt of YOU and relate to you, OR to choose another vendor who is a better fit. (Remember, that's totally OK! Because NO Brand is UNIVERSAL!)

This is a good thing! Because, when you are crystal clear on the makeup of your Personal Brand, you begin attracting those who are in alignment with it! You might've already experienced the struggle of working with a client or customer who is not aligned with your Brand —it's stressful and will often pull you out of alignment. It often takes twice the work and effort, for the same amount of ROI, right? Our goal is to keep this from happening by attracting those who are aligned with your value position, and giving you the "spidey sense" to discern whether or not to work with them from the get-go!

I know, this is a lot of work on you, something you may not be accustomed to, but I invite you to continue your trust in this process. Your awakening to your own Personal Brand power could unlock all kinds of opportunities, smarter more strategic decisions, and powerful manifestations due to your clarity. It's the Law of Attraction plain and simple.

So, remember to carve out specific time on your calendar to dig in and keep up the great work. Your Personal Brand Presence DNA is coming more and more alive after each chapter!

What percentage of your customers want to be loyal?

- a) 18%
- b) 35%
- c) 72%
- d) 94%

Source: Zamba Solutions

Did you guess, **d) 94%?** That's the correct answer! And it is in our favor as a solo-professional or leaders (think of "customers" as "followers'or employee team). People truly want to trust who they are hiring or "buying into," we just sometimes give them reasons not to. And we don't even realize the little things that build up in an experience time and time again that erodes the trust and buy-in enough to "force" the client or follower to leave!

An example of this statistic is how I felt when a vendor I used was consistently late for our scheduled appointment. Even though I was always 5-10 minutes early, she was often 15-30 minutes late. As a customer, I let it continue for too long, getting frustrated every time I made an appointment, but I kept hoping it would get better. I dropped a few comments here and there, but she never caught on. And I certainly didn't want the headache and spend the time trying to replace this vendor (at the time that pain was bigger than my actual frustration). But, eventually the continued disregard of my time eroded my trust. So, I was open to receiving the contact information of a different vendor from a close friend. You know what I did? Yes, I called them and set an appointment. The first vendor lost my business because she didn't respect my time, nor was she concerned about the retention of a recurring customer—me.

Before we move on, consider whether you think this statistic is relevant to your customers, friends, and colleagues. None of us have the time to go searching for someone else to trust and commit our dollars to. It's funny that sometimes we do everything we can as customers to justify staying loyal, because we just don't want the hassle of finding another resource. But when it comes down to it, you've got to leave, don't you? You deserve better service and better care. And so do your customers. Those vendors who care about being congruent to their Brand promise are out there and waiting for your patronage! Just like your clients are waiting for you, that is YOUR competitive advantage!

Everyone is uniquely different, it's time to uncover and realize your power of connection!

Lesson 1: Uncovering Your Authentic Distinction

GETTING BEYOND THE SURFACE

If you are meeting with someone for the first time and you've never seen them before, you will often want to know how to recognize them. That person may say "I'm the one who is wearing the purple tie and yellow shirt."

For this exercise, you will be practicing looking below the surface. Using more than visual clues to identify who they are and capture the subtle characteristics that arise as you get to know the person that formed these perceptions over time. These are Personal Brand Attributes that we can categorize as differentiators. They aren't the type of statistics we would call "demographics" but are closer to what we would call "psychographics"—this data reveals the cognitive factors that drive human behaviors. This includes emotional responses and motivations; moral, ethical, and political values; and inherent attitudes, biases, and prejudices, even interests and hobbies.

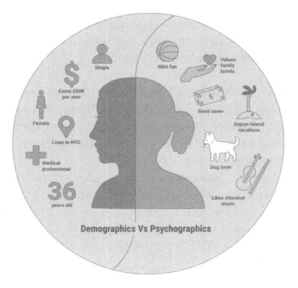

Demographics Vs Psychographics

Source:
https://www.cbinsights.com/research/what-is-psychographics/#what

When you pick up on psychographic data through conversation and observation, it creates a distinction in your mind, such as a feeling of credibility, trust, sensing unique abilities of that person, resonance or dissonance to how they are presenting information, and so much more.

As you listen to people talk, start recognizing their personality traits, skill sets, their points of view, and other nuances that begin to distinguish them from others that you know.

Here are two examples of this process.

"GRETCHEN" says...

> "...I was a competitive volleyball player, I love bright colors, staying busy, and playing games. I am now CEO of Workplace Playground and always looking for ways to help make work more fun for my clients."

What can you assimilate are some of Gretchen's Personal Brand Style attributes?

Here's another example.

"TODD" mentions...

> "...I tend to break down a problem into smaller bytes until I find the best solution...have a degree from MIT, I love taking things apart and putting them back together again...and I moonlight as a comedian."

What, just from these short dialogues, could you guess they valued?

So, getting beyond the surface by assessing true distinction from a psychographic standpoint is a fun, exploratory process as you meet and get to know others through conversation and narrative. It is like you are a detective picking out details and piecing them all together to formulate a perception of that person as you are fed more and more multi-sensory information from them.

Now, "DEREK's brief information reveals his highly intellectual capacity and desire for knowledge and community contribution.

"...I have two undergrad degrees and a PhD, am co-chair of an alumni committee and on the PTA board as well as a grade school soccer coach."

"SARAH" loves numbers and I bet she leans into expecting accuracy in the world around her. She has a caring nature and wants to help others while being competitive and probably a great leader and coach. Let's look at her narrative.

"...Eight years in business finance, I volunteer as an EMT, and am coach of a girls Little League baseball team."

These are all very revealing examples and are designed to help you notice the nuances in their conversations at a very conscious level.

All these short example dialogues are revealing powerful personal differentiators and they can each be leveraged to showcase more of their authentic self as they get more familiar with their own Personal Brand Presence DNA. By being more aware, they can consciously, strategically, and deliberately create consistencies that build trust over time.

Your Personal differentiators are detailed characteristics and experiences that set you apart from others. They enhance and add to what you bring to your customers, family, friends, and colleagues. They create an exponential depth to the understanding of who you are by others. And by recognizing them in yourself, you create a powerful consciousness of your own value position.

Detailed characteristics that can set you apart include:

- Degrees
- Certifications
- Years of experience
- Breadth of experience
- Niche knowledge
- Skill sets
- Life events
- Subjects matter expertise

- World views/Philosophies
- Hobbies/Interests/Passions
- Volunteer work
- Languages spoken
- Musical instruments played

Think of all the assets you have to bring to the credential table to exemplify your Personal Brand. Your differentiators enhance what you bring to your audience.

Personal Brand differentiation example – "Jerry"

Jerry was a college dean who I worked with and wanted to build a business training department he ran at a local institution. Jerry was essentially "the Brand" representing his department and he felt he needed to realize what he was bringing to the table in order to effectively position and sell the unique training services he provided to local businesses.

With some fun brainstorming and a guided process, this is what he came up with:

- Resource for hundreds of leading practice strategies
  Proven three-Step Proprietary Process for Behavioral Change
- Access to 2.7 M in grant money
- Dean with three College Degrees
- 50+ years combined experience in professional and academic environments
- 19 years as international speaker
- 28 years training/facilitation experience
- Guaranteed results
- Awarded Marketing Educator of the Year
- Customer-Rated 3.9 on 4.0 scale for "Wow" factor
- Trained over 32 companies in Colorado Springs, Colorado

Notice how putting numbers (quantifiers) in his differentiators adds to the robustness of his credentials. Quantifying yours with any kind of numbers/statistics can provide a great advantage in how you are perceived by your audiences.

Jerry says "...the process was very thought-provoking and enabled me to see myself in a new light. I was able to resurrect the value of my past experiences and apply them into my daily life creating a unique positioning statement. It was truly affirming for myself to realize all the credentials I do have in my field, and as a person who can impact others in positive ways.

Now, I can feel that you're thinking, "Wow, I don't have as many credentials as Jerry does..." Well he has lived an entire career (he was about 62 when I worked with him). And know, that if you dig deep enough, you will find you have some amazing experiences that showcase your own unique differentiators. Everybody does, and you are not an exception! We often disregard real differentiators because we are so close to it, it doesn't feel different to us. But when you go through the exercise, let go of your own judgements and list all the things that come up for you. You can always go back and hone them. Just getting them all down on paper is a powerful way to affirm your value position, experience, and the impact you can have on your audiences.

So, have some fun with this, recognize the nuances in how you think, what you tend to do better than others, and what skill sets and talents you bring to the table!

> *Quick story:* I was presenting a workshop for a local business association to an audience of about 60, teaching them about the difference between the function of marketing and the function of Branding. Somehow, I started telling a story about when my husband and I were on the river fly fishing one day and how we developed a communication ritual when we suddenly got a fish on the line and we were far away from each other, sometimes around the bend and out of sight from one another. It was a funny story to illustrate a specific point. But after the workshop, a woman came up to me and was so excited about what she learned in the workshop and that she was a fly fisherwoman! She couldn't believe I was one as well and at that

moment connected with me in a way that resonated with her and she said, "You and I are going to work together to build my Personal Brand!"

Sometimes the connections we create with communicating our skill sets, experiences, and even hobbies can fast track trust and open doors to relationships that may never have happened due to the coherence that occurs deep within our hearts from this knowledge!

Here's another example of a Personal Brand client list of differentiators: Meet Julie, 50-years-old, reinventing herself and career. And to get to know here even more, her set of Brand Style attributes are: PRACTICAL, ENERGETIC, CLASSY but SPLASHY, and LOYAL.

1. **Teacher:** Twenty-five years of experience in high school and higher education; expert in presentation, creation, facilitation, and leading.
2. **Author:** Two training manuals - one for new consultants in a direct selling company (adornable.u), one for facilitators at a leadership ranch (the J. Kyle Braid Leadership Foundation, now the JKB Experiential Education Foundation).
3. **Volunteer:** Eighteen years facilitating in a volunteer role for leaders in high schools. Worked with nearly 700 participants in this role over the years.
4. **Experiential trainer:** Facilitating, teaching, and training have made me an expert at interactive, fun, collaborative, and creative workshops.
5. **Degrees:** M.A. in Human Speech Communication - How we interact with others on an interpersonal, group, and corporate level.
6. **Creator:** Reinvention of myself in successful careers. Teacher, brain trainer, gifted and talented coordinator, home-business owner, and leader, creating my own business.
7. **Competitor:** Skied competitively for Fourteen years, played piano competitively for six years, ran races for twenty years (5k-1/2 marathons).
8. **Entrepreneur:** Eight years with national distributor company.
9. **Entrepreneur:** Productivity Expert/Consultant, Speaker.

10. Loves to Karaoke! Won Regional Karoake award.

Once she had completed this exercise, Julie commented, *"I am now realizing my depth of knowledge and value I bring to my new entrepreneurial endeavor as a productivity expert. I want to list these on my business website to enable others to know more about me at a deeper level and connect with who I am and how I am different than others in my industry."*

She has experience and skill sets from her past that she can now pull from and leverage in her new career. Some of these have nothing to do with her current industry, but everything to do with shaping our perceptions of the type of person she is. Getting all these differentiators listed and acknowledged is a powerful exercise to identify and define your value position and what you can bring to the table in relationships with others going forward. It gives you top of mind talking points, infuses you with confidence, and provides your audiences an opportunity to connect with you at a variety of levels.

This chapter is a personal study in the incremental details that make you who you really are. It is an opportunity to appreciate where you've been and what you've accomplished. It forces you to reflect on your past, think about how you've evolved, and create desires for your future. Do not discount the intrinsic value that goes into efforting through this exercise.

> **Fair Warning!:** *You might just start falling back in love with who you really are.*

When you do this and all of these exercises with intention, you are opening the doors to become your full human potential. Enabling yourself to be more internally driven, rather than externally impacted. That is transformational.

It is perfectly normal to feel uncomfortable at first, especially if you feel like this activity encourages "bragging" or self-promotion. Some people have more trouble with this type of exercise than others and that's totally okay. I can assure you that this is not bragging. It is about self-recognition, self-authorship, and self-love and appreciation. It is going to let your unique gifts shine through and be accurately represented in your Brand.

Be proud of who you are and what you've done to get to this place in your life.

Remember, Buddha said, "Your purpose in life is to find your purpose, and live it fully!"

Identifying your unique differentiators (personal and business) opens the doors for deeper human connection and relevance to your market.

You can ponder your Personal Brand differentiators by looking at all aspects of your skill sets. Think of all the assets you must bring to the credential table and to exemplify in your Personal Brand.

THESE "SKILL SETS"/Experiences CAN INCLUDE:

- Educational degrees
- Certifications
- Years of experience
- Breadth of experience awards
- Philosophy
- Unique talents
- Languages spoken
- Volunteer experience
- Travel experiences
- World views
- Authorship
- The first ever...
- The only...
- Cancer survivor

When you take the time to flush out your skill sets, you will come up with some surprising results. Ones that you haven't thought of consciously or thought to leverage in this way. Your experiences shape who you are and your Personal Brand and can be leveraged in many ways. But only if you acknowledge them first.

When my clients realize the extent of their own differentiators, they begin to see themselves as worthy of the perfect client. It enables them to remember how experienced they really are, what they bring to the table, and feel an up-leveling in their confidence. This exercise helps to re-energize your passions, justify your experience, and carve out new paths toward your next evolution.

I am thrilled you are here. Keep up the work, realize the mental and heart-centered shifts in your demeanor and self-narrative, and surrender to what is becoming within you.

LET'S RECAP!
- Now that you know what you know about differentiation, are you curious to find out what yours are?
- Let's determine your differentiators: Define Your Personal Brand Differentiators Exercise #1 -
  - Schedule 1 hr. quality time and review examples.
  - Identify at least five unique Personal Brand Differentiators.

Details are powerful! Incorporate factual numbers, stats, and percentages wherever applicable! Use the list of key areas for your brainstorming processes.

[See Brand Exercise Ch3/1, Page 143
– Identify & Define Your Unique Differentiators.]

So, how do you feel about your work in Chapter 3? I bet you didn't realize how many differentiators you actually had and how you can begin to leverage them in what you do and how you show up with confidence and clarity to your "audiences!"

"Some of the coolest dreams that ever came true weren't dreams at all, but STANDARDS that were never compromised!"

-THE UNIVERSE www.TUT.com

———

CHAPTER 4

YOUR STANDARDS SET THE STAGE FOR LIVING YOUR POTENTIAL!

Tolerance. What is it? Do you have it? How can realizing it and adjusting it change your world?

> **Tolerance:** *The capacity to endure or allow something to continue in your experience.*

I bring this term up because it has everything to do with your next exploration within this chapter. We are going to be getting conscious about your current environment that you are tolerating. It is about taking more control of what you want, expect, and deserve. It is about the beginnings of transforming how you will manifest your experiences in six different areas of your life.

When you become more conscious, strategic, and deliberate in, first, WHO you are, and second, WHAT you want and expect, you can literally become the designer of experiences that align with them. And setting standards for your "future present state" will open the doors to enabling you to begin to live those standards at exponential levels.

I ask you to trust the process of these lessons and exercises. Dive in as if your future life depended on it. Think creatively, think big, and allow your heart to express all that it knows to be true about you. Carve out time now on your calendar to allow this process to work through you, standard by standard that you define, supportive action by supportive action that you set, and you will begin to reap the benefits of your power to pre-pave your future.

You've got this.

Lesson 1: Define Your Personal Brand Standards of Living & Supportive Actions

Your Personal Brand exists well beyond your professional environment. Most of us don't think about ourselves in each area of our lives as separate, but we often show up that way because of the nature of our deep desire to adapt to our surroundings (being easily externally impacted). But, if you think about it, acting different in different circumstances is against our natural way of being. Most of us have "learned" to assess our environments and taught ourselves to adjust to it in order to fit in. Whether it is our best interest or not. Whether we are fully aligned with who we really are or not. This can be dangerous to our well-being. And, in my opinion, is unsustainable longterm. It can chip away at our internal happiness because we are not living our authentic selves to our fullest.

> *In Social Psychology the need to belong is an intrinsic motivation to affiliate with others and be socially accepted.*
> [1] *This need plays a role in a number of social phenomena such as self-presentation and social comparison.*
>
> *1. Schneider ML, Kwan BM. . Psychol Sport Exerc. 2013;14(5):776–785. doi:10.1016/j.psychsport.2013.04.005*

I believe that is why most of us, around the age of 40, start questioning who we are and become more curious in our existential search for alignment. We are becoming more conscious of what makes us happy and unhappy and begin to want more from life that is aligned with who we are. But the work has to be done to identify and define us, before we can ever fully align to it. Again, this is true because *clarity is the basis for action.*

Hence, the Personal Brand Standards of Living exercise is designed to hone in on your unique tolerance to the world around you and how you can up-level and align to it. Personal Brand Standards of Living are specifically personal, brand-relevant criteria which you define and use to guide your approach to life events and tasks that you adhere to daily. You are literally writing "standards" to live by based on your Personal Brand Values and Style Attributes.

Defining these standards in six key areas of life is a journey in and of itself. It encompasses the following areas:

Each one of these "standards areas" are pivotal in refining how you want to up-level your world. I have separated each of these into their own exercise so that you can segment your time separately for each one and digest the meaning of each for yourself. I encourage you to be thoughtful in these exercises and reflect on what you know to be true within each standard declaration and what future state you desire.

You will see yourself through the lens of these dimensions and more readily live into the declaration they outline once you acknowledge the strength of your Personal Brand as the foundation of your life. These are all standard levels of belief you hold yourself up to in the world. Although this process isn't easy, it is thought-provoking and transformational. It should flow as you dig deeper and become more authentic and reveal what makes you, YOU, by consciously setting the standards of your Personal Brand to continue to evolve.

"If you want to change your life you have to raise your standards."

- Tony Robbins, Author, Speaker, Coach, Consultant

How do *Standards of Living* tie into the work you did in Chapters 1 and 2? Each Standard of Living you compose is inherently tied to your core values and style attributes. As you write these sections, take a look at the definitions of your attributes and glean how one or more of them shows up more prominently within each Standard. Think of setting your Standards of Living as crafting a powerful declaration for that part of your life, as if you were authoring it into existence, predisposing yourself to a particular way of experiencing that area of your life. You are the author, you get to lay the ground work and design it to align to your Values and Style.

In a moment, I will provide you with some examples of these Standards of Living "declarations" from my graduate clients, but first, I want to get you clear on the second part of the Standards exercise. Setting up your Supportive Actions for each Standard you compose.

This process is about identifying and then becoming who we say we are with resilience and consistency and this exercise helps you to break it out into bite-size pieces in accordance to different areas of your life. You must really WANT it to become it and take action for this to truly serve you.

A question is often raised during the Personal Brand Presence DNA process. What is the difference between a goal and a standard?

GOAL: (Your Supportive Actions should be written as goals.) Statement of intent; a performance target to be achieved.

Example: "Lose 10 pounds by xx date," or "Save $5,000 for a retirement account by the end of the year."

These actions/goals have a beginning and an end to them (until the next goal is set). They are time-bound. Once achieved, you can set another goal/Supportive Action, in order to continue advancing your way of being to match your Standard of Living declaration.

STANDARD: (Declaration of your belief and way of being.) It sets a normal and customary level of performance excellence reflected in your everyday life actions and behaviors.

Your declaration should include answers to questions like, 'How I relate and stay in touch with my family. How I manage my finances. How I practice my spirituality or contribute to my community' (relevant to each of the 6 areas).

WORTH REFLECTING: *If you've ever worked in corporate America, you might be familiar with the term "Key Performance Indicators" or KPI for short. You can think of your Standards of Living like a set of KPIs for your life!*

What does a finished Standard of Living and Supportive Actions look like?

Let's look at how my client, Phoenix is infusing her attributes into her Standards of Living declarations. We'll take some of her Brand Values and Style attributes and see how she instills them into her philosophy within three (of the six) areas of her Standards of Living scorecard.

Remember, there are two parts to this exercise, the second part to this lesson is to establish some SUPPORTIVE ACTIONS around your overall Standard of Living declarations. These are designed for you to simply pin-point specific, actionable goals that can be accomplished that will enhance how you are living your Personal Brand Standard in each of the areas. You'll notice that the supportive actions are written with a deadline or some level of quantifiable number. This detail is important to inspire the right, aligned action and get and keep you inspired to walk your talk!

Phoenix is owner a Travel Agency—here are three Standards of Living examples:

WORK: I have chosen the field I want to work and play in. I love to help people explore the world with their senses. To be able to see, touch, smell, hear, taste, and experience what we read about in books. I help people see that the world isn't as far away as they think, that travel is possible, and doesn't have to be scary or out of reach. I am a learner at the core. I continuously work to improve my knowledge of suppliers, vendors and places through education, certifications, and training. My goal is to open the eyes, ears, and taste buds of my clients and enable them to fully experience the world around them with wonder and inspiration.

Values/Style attributes aligned: Education, Adventurous

Supportive Actions:

1. Complete my "Master Viking Certification" program by the end of February.

2. Enroll and complete the Travel Leaders Certification as a Luxury Specialist—completed by May 1st.

3. Continuously work to find the best pricing, accommodations, and service for my clients: on-going.

4. Book my next excursion and document with vlogs and Facebook posts for my prospects and clients to experience my own trips—by April 15th.

5. Develop a "sensory questionnaire" for my clients to complete before I dive into planning their ultimate travel experience - April 1st.

FAMILY: My husband is my best friend, my confidant, and support partner in everything. We work hard so we can play hard. We support each other in all things. We are intentional about carving out time to spend together. We regularly communicate what we want to do next and celebrate our accomplishments. I value our mutual compassion and respect for each other and sustain it through our trust and commitment.

Values and Style Attributes aligned: Respect, Compassion, Inquisitive

Supportive Actions:

1. Scheduled day dates and weekend play dates, concerts, hiking, travel, activities, etc. by the last Sunday of each month for the following month.

2. Continue to find new and fun things to do together, one time a week, explore new restaurants and places close by.

3. Every six months sit down for 1 hour to talk about our goals for the next six months. And map out a plan to accomplish them.

———

WORTH REFLECTING: Notice how well Phoenix creates key detailed supportive actions/goals to coincide and support her written Standard of Living to be true and continue to perpetuate it. The supportive actions have goal dates and details to keep track of her progress and accomplishments.

Next, Phoenix works on her Mind/Body Standard of Living and creates this declaration about that area of her life.

MIND/BODY: It is important that I can be physically present in all the activities that I do around the world, hiking up Machu Picchu, scuba diving the Dominican Republic, walking around Europe, and so much more. My health is my wealth! It is about being leaner, having more energy, and feeling my best! Being fit and strong supports my desire to have more clarity and focus. My body loves motion and my mind thrives on clarity, and use yoga as a movement practice to help invigorate my mind and body.

Values and Style attributes aligned:
Education, Compassion, Respect, Adventurous

Supportive Actions:

1. Start 365 days of yoga on January 1st.

2. Incorporate my shakes and nutrition plan January 1st—I have a supportive group and a nutritionist that I am working with to keep me on track.

3. I walk two miles three times a week with a neighbor friend.

Notice how her Standards of Living statements are truly "declarations'as to how she wants to set up each of those areas in her life to align with her Personal Brand.

You can see how she is applying her relevant Personal Brand Values and Style Attributes to her Standards of Living scorecard areas. You can apply as many of your Values and Style Attributes as you want to create powerful, well-rounded, and robust Standards of Living statements. Don't be afraid to push the envelope and go beyond what you are currently experiencing in life. Get inspired to "author" a new, next level of being in each standard so that you can begin to step into your alignment more and more and experience it becoming more tangible.

This exercise will help you infuse and elevate the level of congruency in how to live your life according to your unique Personal Brand DNA. It's all about actioning what you say you believe in.

Try doing one area a day or just a few a week so that you can have time to contemplate your declaration and supportive actions with true robustness. This is where the magic and action begin to show up and help your Brand DNA become more tangible in your experience.

Your Personal Brand Standards of Living should not remain static. This is another area that will evolve as you elevate your Personal Brand actions. As you begin living more consciously with your Personal Brand values and style, you will find new ways to improve on and leverage as changes in your life mature.

You'll want to continue to review and enhance your Standards of Living to not only reflect life changes, but to stimulate new supportive actions to affirm your Brand and keep it aligned with your own evolution.

Your Standards of Living should be reviewed and updated at least annually if not semi annually.

Your Personal Brand Standards of Living are designed around your Brand Values and Style Attributes. They are composed to get you to become highly focused on how you want to live in alignment with what you believe, and what actions you will commit to take to make that happen. This is all a part of your efforts to complete this process of creating a solid, clearly articulated Personal Brand roadmap that is traveled throughout every facet of your life.

Know the difference between alignment and misalignment.

I'm sure you have met people who always claim they are one thing, but their actions often aren't congruent with what they are saying to you. This type of behavior can quickly lose trust in relationships. It affects your advancement and collaborations at work and creates mistrust in personal relationships too. When you experience this, you are dealing with a situation called *Cognitive Dissonance.*

> **Cognitive Dissonance:** *Occurs when the perception is no longer congruent with a person's experience (i.e. I thought I was going to experience this a certain way because of what I think I know about the person, but my experience was different).*

This is the opposite of *Cognitive Resonance*, which occurs when the perception matches the person's experiences. Resonance provides a feeling of value, alignment, and contentment. You get what you expected and things make sense.

By understanding the difference between the two, I'd like you to be very conscious of them in how you perceive yours and others' actions. Pay close attention to how you experience it and the dissonance or resonance you feel in your gut. Review your Personal Brand Values and find areas where you can resonate more with your actions and behaviors. Be more congruent with who you say you are—that will create consistencies that build trust and deepen relationships.

Your Personal Brand authenticity will be sharpened and clarified exponentially when you are conscious of Brand resonance versus dissonance. It's the Law of Attraction.

When should you commit to your own clarity and alignment?

I came across this study below about life regrets collected by a hospice worker and felt even more compelled to pen this book now (among all the other training I have been creating over the past 17 years). Because the more we uncover and understand about ourselves, the more power we have to BE ourselves and own our happiness.

See if any of these statements from hospice patients resonate with you currently, take action to avoid reflecting on these same thoughts on your own death bed someday.

TOP FIVE LIFE REGRETS (told to a hospice worker):
1. I wish I hadn't WORKED so hard.
2. Wish I'd stayed in touch with my FRIENDS.
3. I wish I'd let myself be HAPPIER.
4. I wish I had the courage to express my TRUE SELF.
5. I wish I had lived a life true to my DREAMS instead of what others expected of me.

Source: Bronnie Ware, 'The Top Five Regrets of the Dying - A Life Transformed by the Dearly Departing'.

Sadly, if you look at the list, the last three items (Happier, True Self, and Dreams) are all regrets that could have been diminished if they had been more self-actualized and leveraged their Personal Brand.

Commit now to not letting these *be your last regrets.*

72

Being conscious of your Personal Brand is the key to managing it effectively. Always put yourself in your audience's shoes, who experience your Brand through all their senses: Sight, smell, taste, hearing, touch, and intuition. And ask yourself, "Was I aligned enough for the 'receiver' of my intentions to be in full resonance with who I am and what I stand for?"

Conscious Personal Branding is understanding that everything you do either contributes to or takes away from the perception others have of your Personal Brand!

Becoming more conscious, strategic, and deliberate with your Personal Brand will help you focus on making sure that everything in your business and life will be uniquely branded as it impacts perceptions others have of you.

See how much fun the process of intentional BRANDING can be? Again, this is simply a refined process that enables you to identify, define, and then align to your best self! With this clarity, you should start to trust yourself more, be more inspired to follow through with your decisions and really show up out there to deliver on your WHY!

I bet you've already run across situations where you say to yourself "Well, that's not really my Brand," or "Yes, that is exactly in alignment with who I am!" This is a result of your conscious clarity and building of your keen awareness of your unique Personal Brand. And because of that clarity, you can be more internally driven versus externally impacted by all that stuff going on around you!

LET'S RECAP!

"In the absence of a distinctive Brand **experience, you** become a **commodity** in the minds of your audience members." —adapted from *The Experience Economy*:

Everything you do either **contributes to** or **takes away** from the perception others have of your Brand.

- Schedule two hrs. quality time & review the Standard of Living examples.
- Identify an overarching personal declaration in each one of the six Standard of Living areas.
- Identify the Value and Style Attributes your Standards declarations are primarily representing and exemplify.
- Identify three-five detailed supportive actions/goals for each Standard of Living area making sure to set a quantifier (time deadline, quantity, etc.) when possible. These are your "baby steps" you commit to doing to further align with your declared standard.

[See Brand Exercises Ch4/1a-1f, Pages 147-153
- Establishing Your Personal Brand Standards of Living.]

What did you learn in Chapter 4?
1. What is the set of specific Brand relevant criteria that guides your approach?
   a. Standards of Living
2. What are the six areas of your Standards of Living Scorecard?
   a. Work, Family, Financial, Community, Mind/Body, Relationships
3. What is the difference between a GOAL and a STANDARD?
   a. Goals include specificity (date/time/amount/etc.) and a quantifier and a deadline to accomplish.
   b. Standards establish a specific "way of being" that becomes the "norm."

"The privilege of a lifetime
is to become
who you really are."

-Carl Jung, Swiss Psychiatrist &
Psychoanalyst

———————

CHAPTER 5

THE SECRET POWER OF MANTRA & KNOWING YOUR "WHY"

Ommmmmmmm! Ahh, Ommmmmmm, Ahh... just getting into my Personal Brand Mantra! Do you want to know what mine is?

My Personal Brand Mantra: "CONSCIOUSNESS, INSPIRATION, and GROWTH!"

These words are powerful to me and motivate me to align to who I really am. I use my Personal Brand Mantra and my WHY statement, which you will be developing in this chapter, to re-align and remind myself of my authentic power.

I've seen stats claiming that the average person gets inundated with over 60,000 messages (stimuli) a day. We are a society of collective overwhelm and are regularly pulled in different directions. By now, as a savvy entrepreneur, you know the value of self-care, even though you may not be that good at it!

Our sympathetic nervous systems are running on high 90% of our days and it is becoming a concerning situation. It's time, in my opinion, to take control of our lifestyles, reflect more, go deeper inside, be more still, more often, and benefit from the process of calibration.

> **PERSONAL CALIBRATION:** *The realigning, through conscious internal awareness, of your perspective toward the truth of who you really are to enable the natural raising of your vibration to perpetuate your full potential.*

Think of these next two lessons as developing a couple of key tools that can bring you back into your authentic self when you need a little reminder—as we all do from time to time! The magic they have when you use them is amazing, I will admit. My clients even say they are transformational. Once you compose them, and ensure they truly resonate, they will have the power to shift your vibration almost instantly and get you back into alignment. It's a feeling of release, a sort of reminder or permission to just be you.

Your personal power elevates as you "remember" who you really are.

But like every tool, we use it to get the benefit out of it. You've already done the heavy lifting of identifying and defining your core Personal Brand Attributes in your DNA, so these two exercises should come easily! Again, give yourself the time to work on your mantra and WHY statements and have some fun with it.

All the information you need is already in you from the work you've already done in this program! I even have some examples for you to peek at! You've got this!

The time spent now on your professional and personal self by getting crystal clear on what you stand for, will all have huge payoffs as you begin to action your unique Personal Brand Presence DNA, your mantra, and your individual "why" positioning statement.

This chapter pulls together your entire Personal Brand Presence DNA into a solid foundation for you to begin creating tangible actions right away.

Ever since I was exposed to Dr. Suess I've always resonated with the five lessons below and wanted to share it with you to kick off the learning in this chapter:

FIVE Lessons in Life from Dr. Seuss®

1. Today you are YOU, that is truer than true. There is no one alive who is You-er than you.
2. Why fit in when you were born to stand out?

3. You have brains in your head. You have feet in your shoes. You can steer yourself any direction you choose.
4. Be who you are and say what you feel, because those who mind don't matter and those who matter don't mind.
5. Today I shall behave as if this is the day I will be remembered.

As you work on acknowledging your distinction so that you are not a "commodity" in the minds of your market and community circles, you will begin to create a memorable mark in others' minds about who you are and what you stand for. Pre-paving the way for trust, collaboration, and advocacy.

Upon Completion of Chapter 5 you will:

1. Compose and leverage your unique Brand mantra that:
   • Energizes and motivates you to focus and re-engage being your best self.
2. Declare and commit to your unique Brand "why" that:
   • Sets structure for leveraging your way of being to the fullest.
   • Gets you laser-focused to deliver consistently On-Brand.

Lesson 1: What Is a "Personal Brand Mantra?"

Have you ever gotten goose bumps from hearing a phrase, quote, something in a speech, or a lyric from a song? We all have at one time or another. You immediately repeat it in your mind and want to store it into your long-term memory because it caused a visceral igniting of your soul. I love it when that happens. And now it happens a lot to me because I am such an appreciator of thoughtful, meaningful, and compelling dialogue—I've been known to call myself a "wordologist."

I believe our *words create our worlds*. Now, how easy is that!

And mantras, especially those composed from deep in our core being, are designed to ignite emotion, flutter our heart, and even well up a tear or two. Mantras are tools of affirmation, appreciation, and remembrance of who we are. They create emotion because they have the ability to wake us up in an instant and pull us back into alignment —the emotion is a result of becoming aware that we were out of alignment and are now being "called back home."

Mantras create a level of comfort, like a warm fuzzy blanket, a bubble bath, or fresh baked brownie out of the oven! They initiate a psychological, vibrational, and emotional shift that enables us to realize what is true for us and pivot back into ease and flow.

> **A short excerpt from Yoga International on Mantras:**
> *The power of mantra is not limited by time, space, or causation, for mantra is a self-existent, self-luminous reality that can be heard by all who have ears to hear. But mantra transcends sound for, as the scriptures say, mantras are seen by the eyes of the soul rather than heard by the ears.*
>
> *https://www.yogainternational.com/article/view/the-power-of-mantra*

Now that you know how I feel about using mantras as a tool, I hope you can get excited about creating yours. It will be powerful, but only if you use it regularly! Think of it as expressing the culmination of your Personal Brand Presence DNA in a short, yet robust few words that you can easily remember and fully resonate with.

So far, you've:

- Identified and defined your Personal Brand Values and Style attributes.
- Flushed out some personal differentiators both on a demographic and psychographic level.
- Established some powerful Standard of Living declarations along with practical supportive actions that will inspire you to walk your talk.

Phew! Congratulations on all the deep dive work. It is now time to get into the next step in building the remaining pieces of your Personal Brand Presence DNA—your Mantra and Why statement.

Your Personal Brand Mantra is:

- A personally meaningful statement or series of words that is repeated and is a point of reference to stay "on-brand" through your daily actions and behaviors.
- The fundamental "essence" of who you are, is enduring and timeless and doesn't change with trends or fads.
  - Consistent across every area of your life representing your core essence that is the foundation of your Personal Brand.
  - Action-oriented and inspirational, exciting and engaging you to focus on your authentic self.
  - Derived from the most distinctive attributes of your DNA, usually three to four highly descriptive, impactful words.
  - NOT a tagline! It is an internal reminder of your core Brand essence and speaks only to you to impact your focus, direction, actions, and behaviors.

Here are meaningful examples of powerful mantras that guide these Personal Brands to consciously and authentically, lift and perpetuate who they are in everything they do.

Remember Sarah from Chapter 3, the financial analyst? Her mantra is honed down to its core essence:

Educated. Nurturing. Empowering.

And Larry, the CEO-type who invests in and leads companies through their growth objectives developed a mantra that exclaims:

Competent. Elegant. Leadership.

By reading his mantra, you get a great sense of Larry's Personal Brand and how he wants others to perceive him. And yes, "Elegant" is one of his key words. He is a very precise, particular, and intentional kind of guy who prides himself on the details that make all the difference in creating excellence out of mediocrity.

Remember this is a powerful Brand positioning tool to reacquaint you to who you really are, in a world that is constantly distracting us in many directions. Think of it as a powerful self-recalibration tool.

And Chevy, the leadership facilitator and conductor, got creative and energetic and used an acronym for his mantra:

L.I.F.E. = Leadership. Integrity. Fun. Excellence.

It isn't hard to get a sense of the energy of his Brand from that mantra. But remember, they are not intended to be a tagline in any way. But rather a deeply meaningful and personal affirmative phrase that raises your vibration quickly and helps to pivot you back into your Personal Brand lane.

To see a variety of client mantras and how they leverage them, take a look at this video:

https://www.youtube.com/watch?v=xlZstyW0dV0&feature=youtu.be

Short, meaningful, and motivational—these are great examples of how mantras express your Personal Brand. And what it can do to direct or redirect, refocus or reframe how you live your Personal Brand every day. Use it as a tool, daily, to realign to who you really are.

Make sure that the words you use for your Personal Brand mantra are moving and compelling to you. Meaning you feel a gut response from saying them, and it inspires you to re-engage and elevate your Personal

Brand's way of being in the moment.

Does it pass the GOOSE BUMPS test? A tried and true test of how powerful your mantra is is whether or not you get a visceral response, like goose bumps from reciting it over and over again. So make sure you take the "test" to ensure you've chosen those key terms or the phrase that moves you at the DNA level!

I invite you to watch a video example of a Personal Brand client who expresses what the mantra process has done for her and her leadership and how she uses her mantra to remind her and realign herself— stepping into her potential.

Visit Stephanie J.'s video with this link:
https://youtu.be/O_ijtWo-qQk

Did you see and feel her energy shift as she expressed her experience? Her energy lifted the moment she started talking about her mantra!

Remember, mantras are highly personal. Don't think they are speaking to your audience in any way, but rather speaking to your inner soul, only you. So, get creative, ensure this phrase truly resonates with you to the point of goosebumps. You will KNOW when you feel it is right on.

I know I think of mine and recite it daily—"it brings me HOME and raises my vibration immediately to center my thoughts and surrender from the external goings on around me. I cannot wait to have you experience this tool for yourself.

LET'S RECAP!

- Are there any points that you can relate to Stephanie regarding your Branding process and mantra?
- Do you feel the need to re-engage in your life?
  - Or re-discover your enthusiasm and motivation?
  - Don't forget that your Personal Brand is YOU. Use your Personal Brand Mantra regularly.
    - Recite it when you wake up!
    - Remember it when you are dealing with tough issues/or people.
    - Recount it when you are anxious, nervous, or unsure.
    - Recant in your daily meditation.
    - Print it out and hang it where you will see it daily.
- Let's develop your Brand Mantra. As you have seen, it can be one of the most impactful, developmental areas of your Personal Brand Presence DNA.
- Once you create your Brand Mantra, you are ready to be introduced to the concept of your Brand "why."

[See Brand Exercise Ch 5/1, Page 154
– Crafting Your Personal Brand Mantra.]

Lesson 2: Identify & Define Your Personal Brand "Why"

"Why am I here?" is, I believe, the second most asked question in humankind...trailing just behind the number one—"Who am I?"

Your Personal Brand Presence work so far has helped you clarify the number one question, now it's time to focus on the second question of humankind.

So many of us get to a point in life where these questions become a quest. We start reflecting on them often and begin a new more focused curiosity that takes us on a journey of new expansion, understanding, and in some instances a new perspective of satisfaction in life. I hope that part of this is why you are here with me inside this process. I hope that your curiosity about yourself is so much more than just the career you've chosen, but that you see an opportunity to create deeper coherence between all of the things you know to be true about yourself.

Did I mention recently how glad I am that you are here?

The building of your Personal Brand Presence DNA needs to have a reason you are creating it. Your "why" is essential. Why do you do what you do? This requires a deeper dive, lots of intention and awareness of your passions.

This lesson is important in helping you to understand and clearly articulate your reason for being. Your "why." You will define and set your own rules for living authentically.

You will craft that into a powerful statement. You will have opportunities to use your Personal Brand Presence DNA attributes throughout the process and end with an authentic declaration for what you will deliver on consistently.

I call this the "Crescendo Concept" within the DNA methodology. This is a declaration detailing the realization of who you are here to become authentically and consciously, through the DNA of your Personal Brand Presence.

It is what you commit to being at every audience touchpoint through your community, relationships, family and how you attend to your mind, body, and financial well-being.

"You are joy-seeking beings who have come forth into what we see as the perfect environment for desire to be born within you. What your work is about is to bring yourself into vibrational harmony with allowing the Energy-that-is-You to flow.

And in simple terms, what that means is: your work is to look - wherever you stand, whether you are looking in the past, present or future - your work is to consume your Now with the thought that feels best."

Abraham Hicks

The focal point of your Personal Brand's "why" is understanding and clearly articulating your reason for being. When this occurs, you get a new disposition to life. You are reengaged and start to dive into your purpose. You'll build a platform for everything you do from this point on.

To identify and define your "why," you will delve into new areas of your Personal Brand Presence DNA.

Your reason for being statement will start with: "I exist to..."

This positions you with power and a broader context to think holistically about who you are.

Why Craft Your Personal Brand's "Why" statement?

- Clearly declares your Personal Brand's orientation which validates what you commit to deliver on every day, in every experience.
- Inspires, energizes, and mobilizes you to create the structures

to perpetuate your authentic "way of being."
- Acts as a "sanity check" to drive your daily decision-making, actions, and experiences to ensure you are living in alignment with your Personal Brand Presence.

You need to know there are consequences to your Brand when you define your "why" and then neglect it.

Once you begin to undermine your "why," then you will start to erode the credibility of your Brand, causing cognitive dissonance and distrust in the minds of your audience. Be prepared to step into your Brand 'why' statement—feel it, live it, be it.

These two important pieces within your Personal Brand DNA profile— your Brand mantra and your Brand 'why' are tools to help keep you authentic and distinctive by being highly conscious in your efforts to live more "on-Brand."

Here are examples of Personal Brands that we knew and trusted and were undermined and disintegrated in the marketplace, at one point in their lives, by losing sight of what was important.

Tiger Woods. Martha Stewart. Lance Armstrong. Each of them paid and may still be paying a price by falling out of alignment with the Personal Brand they worked so hard to create and live up to. The result of their fall was partly in choosing not to live up to their Brand values, their Brand Style and fully commit to their "why" of who they represented to the public and who they believed they were.

Although declaring your Personal Brand why is important, keeping it and living up to it consistently is the real test. By adhering to your Brand Why declaration, your home, work, and community audiences will gain clarity on knowing what to expect from you. And trust will continue to build as you evolve into your authentic potential.

Pulling your Brand Mantra and Brand Why out of your toolbox daily will aid you staying top of mind, make you more aligned, help you have more on-Brand decision-making tools and be more consistent to walk your talk.

Let me demonstrate how the Brand Mantra relates to the Brand "Why" statement with the following examples. We went over these Personal Brand Mantras earlier. Now let's add their Brand "Why" statements.

Sarah:
Educated. Nurturing. Empowering.

"I EXIST to inspire higher levels of thinking while being patient and nurturing to encourage empowerment and confidence in those who experience me."

Larry:
Competent. Elegant. Leadership

"I EXIST to exemplify coherence, deliver competence, and be strategically driven to leadership that produces game-changing results within lives I touch in an elegant fashion."

Chevy:
LIFE! = Leadership. Integrity. Fun. Excellence.

"I EXIST to create innovative, inspiring, and memorable environments that empower and perpetuate thoughtful, values-based leadership to evolve and elevate others.

These 'Why' statements coupled with the Mantra are powerful tools they use regularly to stay in alignment and to be inspired to stand in their power. Its highly personal and meaningful to YOU. You can do this too!

LET'S RECAP!

Remember that your Personal Brand is truly all about YOU, not what everyone else thinks you should do and be.

- Uncover what makes you light up in life.
- What if you couldn't ever fail at something? What would you

be doing now?
- Realize dismissed opportunities of the past, while reigniting the defined YOU into your next potential

[See Brand Exercises Ch 5/2, Page 156
– Uncovering Your "Why"]

Lesson 3: Attracting YOUR People and Releasing the Rest

By now, you may be thinking, "My Personal Brand could appeal to everyone!"

This is a dangerous mindset and will only keep you in a state of stress because it cannot occur. Our humanism is vast and so varied that, until you understand and accept that you, yourself, have a unique way of being that will attract like beings, you won't be able to ever satisfy the whole. But there is quantum elegance in that and knowing it!

This exercise is not the time to be considering the "peanut gallery" (all those people/audiences you might be wanting to please, or be liked by, or get approval from). When you consider everyone regarding your Personal Brand, you imprison yourself to behave in ways that are driven from outside of you. Your goal in identifying and defining your Personal Brand Presence is to FREE yourself into your own natural, internally driven alignment.

Your evolution is to become more INTERNALLY DRIVEN vs. EXTERNALLY IMPACTED.

One of the big oversights in building a Brand, whether business or personal, is to think that the Brand is so wonderful it must appeal to all.

> **WORTH REFLECTING:** But even with a Personal Brand as timeless as Martin Luther King, or even Mother Teresa, will never appeal to everyone. Knowing and accepting this will

enable you to start blossoming into who you are by being more conscious, strategic, and deliberate in being INTERNALLY DRIVEN vs. EXTERNALLY IMPACTED.

Take a look at this short excerpt from my ebook, *The 6 Myths of Small Business Branding*.

Myth #5: MY Brand APPEALS TO EVERYONE
Truth #5: NO Brand IS UNIVERSAL!

Are you a PC/Android fan? Are you an Apple/iPhone fan? OK, before we get into the war zone, understand that each Brand has a uniqueness to it that compels a certain audience or market to become loyal, raving fans and even ritualists! There are certain attributes to Mac's that appeal more to the creative types from the distinct design of the physical product, to the detail, color, and aesthetic style of visuals within the platform itself. (Can you tell which one I am a fan of?) Then there is the practical, analytical, look, feel, and logical functioning of a PC.

The learning point here is that there has to be contrast in Brands in order to create distinction within the minds of the market and choices that we all, as consumers, expect and demand! What we, as business owners and employees, need to do is understand the differences, embrace them, and then leverage and capitalize on what those differences are via behavior, product, service, or style!

To pursue this further if Walmart® appealed to everyone, there would be no Target®. For that matter, if JC Penney® appealed to everyone, there would be no Nordstrom®. If McDonald's® appealed to everyone, there would be no Wendy's®, Carl's Jr.®, or Arby's® (not to mention Taco Bell®!) Can you imagine a world without those? How do you think they can all coexist, successfully, in a one-mile stretch of suburbia? Because they each have targeted a specific market and capitalized on the attributes that market demands and spends their hard-earned money on.

You can download this ebook and workbook at:
https://brandascension.com/product/the-6-myths-of-branding-
audio-book-e-book-workbook/

The same can be said for Personal Brands which have their own style and value attributes that appeal to different types of people. Celebrate your uniqueness and who you attract in your life. Learn to embrace your Brand's strengths and leverage them through actions and behaviors in every aspect of your life.

As you gain clarity on your Personal Brand Presence and its uniqueness, you will be more consistent and authentic and instill trust in your circle of influence. You will begin attracting and retaining those who appreciate who you are and what you offer. Most importantly, you will not feel the need to appeal to all audiences nor shift your actions and behaviors to get their buy-in and lose sight of who you are.

Knowing that universal appeal of your Personal Brand is nearly impossible to establish and sustain, think through these questions:

- Think about Personal Brands that appeal to specific audiences and ones that appeal more to the masses.
- Is it more important to you to have a universal appeal and not aligned with your core or creating a Personal Brand that is authentically aligned to you?
- Even though you don't have universal appeal, it doesn't mean you can't create a vast audience of advocates. Brands like Apple were built by a Personal Brand named Steve Jobs. And Starbucks didn't see its exponential growth until Howard Shultz committed his Personal Brand to the company. And we know the vast following Oprah has with her Personal Brand delivery.
- None of these Personal Brands appeal to everyone, but they do have an incredible following of advocates who relate to them and trust them because of their unrelenting consistency to be who they say they are.

Be conscious of your Personal Brand Presence DNA.

Everything you do in your life, contributes to, or takes away from the perception others have of your Personal Brand...It determines how they talk about you and promote you to others. The key today is growing and sustaining your Personal Brand not through traditional marketing vehicles, but rather, through delivering a positively memorable experience. Your audience—including customers—will develop a deep level of trust with you, continue to come back to great lengths to speak favorably about you, support you, and bring new audiences and customers to your door.

The many other benefits to becoming your authentic self can manifest in building confidence, assuredness, feeling more life satisfaction, being more content, and less stressed in the running of your life.

Developing more clarity around who you are is a powerful basis for acting and leveraging your authentic self. And for leading others to do the same.

LET'S RECAP!

- What is a Personal Brand Mantra? It is a brief, motivating statement that represents the fundamental essence of what your Personal Brand stands for.
- It reflects the heart and soul, or essence, of your Brand Presence.
- What is a Personal Brand "Why?" It is a declaration detailing the realization of who you are here to become authentically and consciously, through uncovering the DNA of your Personal Brand Presence.

[See Brand Exercise Ch 5/3, Page 168
– Crafting Your Personal Brand "Why" Statement.]

I use my Brand Mantra a lot! There is so much in our external environments that can get us out of alignment and out of our own lanes – so I use it to bring me back into focus of what I know to be true for me. And you can too!

I hope you can feel your Brand all coming together by now. Remember to complete your Personal Brand Presence DNA one sheet so you have a printable and hangable quick reference sheet to refer to…. I keep mine in my office just beyond my computer screen, so it is always in sight!

I am excited for you and the work you've done so far to complete your Personal Brand Presence. Now it's time to start making it all work for you.

Lesson 4: Taking Action — In Sight, In Mind

It's time for some tangible, actionable ways that you can begin sooner than later in transforming your mindset. This exercise is called 'In Sight, In Mind,' because I believe that the more you see your Personal Brand Presence DNA template, the more you will consciously utilize it.

Complete, print and post your Personal Brand Presence DNA Onesheet in key areas of your workspace, home, etc. (Download from Resources, Page 175).

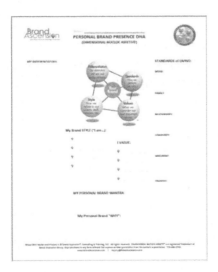

Use It or Lose It!

- Laminate it. Frame it. Honor it.
- Carry with you a mini version of your DNA in your wallet or purse.
- Start the day out with a 60-second review/refresh.
- Consider recording yourself reciting the attributes, your Mantra, and "Why" statement!

This may seem like overkill but studies show that repetition and kinesthetic (the act of doing) is the best way to transfer information into our limbic brains to build our longterm memory. Remember, we are breaking that insanity habit and turning off "auto-pilot" and getting in the driver's seat of our lives. Meaning we are doing something different—to get different results, by being more conscious, strategic, and deliberate.

Here are some more actions to fast track leveraging your Personal Brand Presence DNA now:

1) **Highlight/Add to your Differentiators** - there is always more that you may not have thought of—take one more "swipe" at contemplating all the areas that make you different. Think back several years to what you've accomplished, what you are known for, and where your expertise lies.

2) **Revisit Differentiators often** so that they ring solid and true for you – make a point to find new ways to add to the list. Join clubs, contests, start drafting that book you want to write. Your Personal Brand Differentiators are dynamic and will change and evolve as you do more.

3) **Ask a close friend or colleague** what they see about you that is unique to you.

4) **Quantify your Differentiators** in any way you can. All this means is adding a number or statistic to your Differentiator, like "15 years in the industry" or you have *three* certifications in your field, or you've been on a steering committee for 4 years.

Solo-preneurs should highlight their Differentiators and put them on their website. "Why work with me?" is a great page title. It breaks you out of the pack and shows your audience what is unique about you and your Brand. Think about outlining relevant differences in all of your collateral pieces and customer communication.

Leaders within organizations benefit from these exercises because it creates the "top-of-mind" appreciation of what you bring to the table. It will support you in building confidence and self-esteem to lead and guide your teams to their own greatness!

Taking the time for honoring your achievements, what you know, your super-powers, and experiences will do wonders for how you energetically show up and how others perceive you. It is something we never do enough of these days. Be grateful, and give yourself grace to life your full potential. You are exactly where you need to be, right now.

"EVERYTHING you DO, markets (communicates) a perception."

– Suzanne Tulien,
Brand Clarity Expert,
Brand Ascension

———

CHAPTER 6

BECOMING A WORLD-CLASS PERSONAL BRAND

I bet when you started this journey you never imagined how conscious, strategic, and deliberate a Personal Brand should be, right? I say should, because so many of us don't take this approach to identify, define, and then align to our own Personal Brand so that we can begin to drive it in ways that enable us to showcase our highest potential.

You will soon uncover a layer of characteristics that you will be able to master through your Personal Brand Presence to ensure you are staying in alignment as much as possible, until you get the "muscel memory" locked in!

This chapter is about actioning your Personal Brand Presence DNA into real, tangible behaviors that help to perpetuate the perceptions you want others to have of you and your authentic self. In work, play, family, and community—you can begin to drive your experiences through your core values and style attributes in a more consistent, distinctive, and generative way to build trust, advocacy, and collaboration in your world. All these things will work together to support your overall growth into more and more of who you are.

Enjoy this chapter, carving out the time for quality attention and focus, and emerge feeling ready and inspired to action.

Thanks for being you and continuing the journey of your personal evolution!

Upon Completion of Chapter 6, you will:

1. Leverage the THREE MOST ESSENTIAL CHARACTERISTICS of highly-successful world-class Brands.
2. Build multi-sensory and memorable experiences.

3. Infuse your Personal Brand Presence DNA into your business and skyrocket your success.

Lesson 1: Authentic Personal Brands Endure

In this lesson, you will recognize the resonating characteristics of authenticity. We will explore how authenticity impacts your Personal Brand's ability to endure and leave the type of impression you want to leave for your intended audiences.

Where the Rubber Meets the Road

This is where you are equipped to make your Personal Brand Presence "tangible" and "actionable." This is where you will create the structures and opportunities to live your full potential through the DNA of your unique Personal Brand Presence. It is where you will begin to think about how to up-level your relationships, processes and word use, and how you speak about who you are, hold conversations, and build impactful relationships with others that are "on-brand."

You are now challenged to live with alignment and accountability to show up congruent with your unique Personal Brand Presence outputs and begin nurturing a new and improved conscious self, full of opportunities that continue to evolve.

Here is a great example to position this chapter's learning points. It comes from the perspective of a business Brand, just consider how to apply it to your Personal Brand building actions and increasing your awareness of who you are and how you show up.

According to *Winning Behaviors* by Terry Bacon and David Pugh, "*The Best-in-Class Brands have more than great products and services, a unique business model, and great people. What really distinguishes them is that they OUT-BEHAVE their rivals.*" How so? They:

- Show **more** care, respect, and commitment.
- Are **more responsive** to customer's [audience] needs.
- Devote **more time** to customers.

- Establish processes to **ensure** better customer treatment.
- **Empower** employees to **enhance** customer experience.

Authenticity is a vibration. You can feel it within you. Others can feel it coming from you.

Now that you have your Personal Brand Presence DNA elements defined, you can begin establishing behaviors/practices that represent your specific attributes—your style, core values, differentiators, and standards. Remember, your DNA attributes are your blueprint for defining specific and unique actions to create and more consistently affirm who you are.

I'll now introduce you to three essential practices of a world-class Personal Brand to practice when consciously managing your behaviors. You will be equipped with the tools to continuously enhance and leverage your Personal Brand Presence to reach your potential.

1) BEING AUTHENTIC:

Can you tell if someone is authentic within the first 30 seconds of meeting them? Most of us can. It is a "spidey" sense we are gifted as humans. And when we can tap into it, it benefits us greatly. But what are some of the clues that someone reeks of inauthenticity?

Inauthenticity:

- People who gossip, right out of the shoot.
- People who don't look you in the eyes.
- People who seem uncomfortable in their own skin.

I am sure you can identify a few more inauthentic actions.

So, what does authentic mean? We know it when we see it but let us look at it through the filter of this Personal Brand Presence DNA process. For this purpose, it means:

AUTHENTICITY: Being fully present and in-the-moment with your audience(s), speaking your truth, acting your truth, and staying genuine to your Personal Brand Presence DNA.

Who do you know in your audience that comes to mind when you think of authenticity? You automatically feel different when you think of them, don't you? Authentic Personal Brands endure. Remember, authenticity is about speaking and acting your truth. People who are consistently authentic are more self-actualized.

[Resource: Check out my BrandByte #11 - Personal Brand Alignment video - https://youtu.be/p_3z4oBJefE]

Now, let's find out how you rank yourself in authenticity. This short audit will, when answered honestly, help you uncover where you are not as authentic as you'd like to be and where you are. All of us have pressures around us that can cause breakdowns in our own authenticity and pull us out of our alignment lane. But Personal Brand clarity and awareness are powerful tools to become more and more deliberate of what you are committed to be authentic to and enable your ability to discern in that direction.

Take a quick stab at this short asessment and reflect on where you can improve. Remember, we cannot truly be "authentic" to ourselves until we know who are are!

[See Brand Exercise Ch 6/ 1, Page 161
- Solopreneur Brand Authenticity Audit.]

Now that you've assest your current authenticity, let's review the list of characteristics from Maslow I presented in Chapter 1.

MASLOW'S SELF-ACTUALIZATION CHARACTERISTICS:

1. Acceptance & Realism
2. Problem-centering
3. Sponteneity
4. Autonomy & Solitude
5. Continued Freshness of Appreciation
6. Peak Experiences

It can be a gift to become more self-actualized. As Carl Jung puts it, *"The privilege of a lifetime is to become who you really are."*

Lesson 2: How Your Consistency Is Key to Personal Brand Success

"Consistency builds Trust, Trust creates History, History forms Traditions, Traditions build RITUALS."

- Martin Lindstrom, author of *Brand Sense*

This quote by Martin Lindstrom exemplifies how legacies are built and sustained. What will it take for your Personal Brand to become a ritual, with your family, friends, colleagues, and others? When your Brand becomes a ritual, you have become a Personal Brand leader and you have the prime opportunity to command respect, build loyalty and advocacy.

In this lesson, you will learn the importance of consistency. You'll have the chance to explore whether this essential trait is something that comes naturally to you or whether you require more focused action plans. You will discover that consistency is one of the key actions that develops a world-class Brand.

This critical characteristic is showcased in this poll. Look at this from the human psychological level and you will see how it applies to Personal Brands as much as it applies to business Brands.

Can you guess? In an annual survey on Brands and Branding by experts from top global Brands, what was cited as the most critical aspect of successful Branding? Source: *The Brand Marketers Report, InterBrand*

Is it:

    a) Marketing,
    b) Consistency,
    c) The actual product uniqueness,
    d) Size of budget, or
    e) Innovation?

With **36%** of the vote, ***consistency*** won hands down. The most important thing to create and sustain success is to capitalize on being consistent in your positive, Brand-relevant behavior. We have a desire to trust not only the businesses we deal with, but the people we deal with. So, focusing on your consistencies, or lack thereof, is a powerful use of your time. Take a look at where you can enhance the consistency of your Brand DNA attributes you are uncovering throughout this book. Start there and get creative with it.

For solo-professionals running your own businesses, another point to note from the above survey is that *marketing and advertising only contributes 0.86% to the success of the business.* That's right.

That's less than 1%.

This gets owners really thinking differently about where to spend money and time on their business. It helps them refocus their efforts when building their Brand.

Hence, the next most essential characteristic of a world-class Personal Brand is to be:

2) BEING CONSISTENT:

It is how you are with every step you take and move you make with your Personal Brand.

> **CONSISTENCY:** *Showing up the same way every time,*
> *to walking the talk and being true to your*
> ***Personal Brand Presence DNA.***

Consistency builds trust in the hearts and minds of your audience which enables advocacy. Trust builds Brand equity and loyalty.

Does consistency come naturally to you? Remember, Personal Brands like Lady Gaga, Madonna, and even Cher, Elton John, and even Valentino Liberace (who was the highest paid entertainer in the world from the 1950s to the 1970s! source: Wikipedia), back in the day were *"consistently inconsistent"* in how they showcased their creativity and in their overall look! We were always kept in wonder as to how they'd show up next! (Kind of exciting, eh?)

But, what about you? As much as we think we are consistent, are we really? And where can we improve? Where might we be breaking the trust chain with our clients, friends, colleagues without realizing it?

Consider running a "consistency audit" in how you operate your business. You might be surprised at how consistency can slip through the cracks occasionally. Remember, consistency is one of the key actions that develops a world-class Personal Brand longterm. And it is not just being consistent in how you deliver your services, but rather to think about how you are actually exemplifying and living your Personal Brand Presence attributes.

[See Brand Exercise Ch 6/ 2, Page 162
- Solopreneur Brand Consistency Audit.]

Lesson 3: Cultivating Your Generative Approach

It's a word not used very often in our day-to-day vernacular. But it is a powerful word and I want you to learn how to become more of it at a conscious level. Embodying this characteristic into your Personal Brand Presence DNA will immediately create momentum and direct energies towards your evolution into your highest potential.

The final essential characteristic for building your world-class Brand is:

3) BECOME MORE "GENERATIVE":

GENERATIVE:
*Regularly stepping into the trajectory of **actualization** by consciously enabling my thinking & being towards opportunities in becoming more of my*
Personal Brand Presence DNA.

Embodying this characteristic requires you to generate the structures necessary for you to fully self-actualize. These structures or containers are essential for manifesting on-Brand opportunities within your particular Standards of Living.

Being conscious of being generative keeps you from falling into a "staying in the contractive state," which is where we stagnate. We miss opportunities, cloud our minds with negative, victimizing thoughts that keep us from being co-creators of our essential selves.

The generative practice is essential in consistently creating the evolution of your Personal Brand. Taking on this practice fully will help ensure that you are always seeking ways to become more of who you really are in every area of your world.

You are innately empowered to evolve. So why not get more conscious in allowing it to flow?

Becoming more *Generative* means you are actively:
- Regularly seeking opportunities to evolve further.
- Willing to see different points of view.
- Seeking 'outside the obvious' solutions to barriers.
- Taking strategic risks to realize your potential.
- Building structures and processes to enable you to live your potential.

Realizing when you are in a more *Contractive* state, is when you are:
- Satisfied with where you are.
- Not trusting outside advice or direction.
- Staying within the 'proven' methods to solutions.
- Highly conservative and protective of getting outside of your comfort zone.
- Stay regimented to old ways and blame others for keeping you stagnant.
- Noticing where you are right now and keeping an awareness of these components at any given time can provide you powerful reflective information signaling you to make more

aligned, On-Brand decisions moving forward. Take a moment and notice which area (generative or contractive) you are right now.

Have you worked with someone who would be considered contracted?

- What did it feel like?
- How does it affect others?
- What kind of role does this play in your Brand?
- What exactly does generative look like in actual behaviors?
- Take, for example, Tony Robbins, Coach, author, speaker, and trainer. He has made a highly-successful living leveraging his style attributes to the fullest. If he had completed the style attribute exercise from this book, we could assume his style attributes are possibly:
  - Direct (TRANSPARENT)
  - Authentic
  - Motivating/experiential
  - Thought-provoking

He is not afraid to challenge his audience to take a deep dive and is not afraid to be controversial, to buck the traditional or current way of thinking or to empower those around him to become their true selves. Not only does he evoke questions that result in a generative mindset to his audiences, but he himself has a consistent mindset of generating more of who he is by creating the structures in his life that help to perpetuate and leverage his Personal Brand.

He is constantly growing his own knowledge base to utilizing technology in creative and effective ways to deliver his program.

The question for you is: How can you be more generative in leveraging your style and value attributes? How can you create the structures and space to deliver on your Brand "why" statement? Who can you start connecting with and relating to that will help keep you on the trajectory of growing into your full potential?

I want to share an excerpt from a webinar I created called:

**"3 Reasons Your Brand Isn't Attracting
the Clients You Want...Yet!" (exerpt)** *https://bit.ly/3fFMSf0*

Watch this excerpt of a webinar I did with case study examples of clients leveraging their Personal Brand Presence in tangible ways.

These three cases exemplify the lessons you have just learned. It gives you a snippet of the three characteristics of a successful Brand. And leads you now into a deeper dive of how to apply what you've learned to boost your Brand through your senses.

LET'S RECAP!

This chapter was about the implementation of the Personal Brand Presence DNA you've uncovered for yourself. The three practices of a world-class Personal Brand are applied to your specific attributes in your DNA.

You apply them by realizing where you can be more CONSISTENT, AUTHENTIC, and even GENERATIVE, within each of the Values and Style attributes you assigned for yourself. This is how you will continue to evolve into more and more of who you are within your DNA. This is how you become more conscious, strategic, and deliberate in living in alignment.

This is about being more internally driven, and less externally impacted.

I invite you to reflect deeply on these practices and commit to applying them to the outputs from your exercises and notice what happens!

*[See Brand Exercise Ch 6/3, Page 163
– How You Become More authentic, consistent,
& generative.]*

"Personal Brand alignment is the catalyst for the self-management of your authenticity."

-Suzanne Tulien,
Brand Clarity Expert

———————

CHAPTER 7

ALIGNING YOUR INTERNAL BRAND WITH YOUR EXTERNAL ENVIRONMENT

Now that you've identified and defined your Personal Brand Presence DNA, the name of the game now is ALIGNMENT. I mean, what good is it to be clear on who you are and what you stand for, without taking action to fully step into and live it?

> *WORTH REFLECTING:* Remember, your Personal Brand Presence is just a PERCEPTION. A perception that you get to identify, define and align to, so that your "audience" perceives you in a specific way—a way that is authentic to you. Consciously doing so, enables you to become your own personal brand manager, be more internally driven vs. externally impacted, and evolve more deliberately with intention.

Walking Your Talk

You may have heard that "your current external experience is a reflection or result of your inner alignment." That thought stops some people in their tracks and there is an immediate resistance to the belief of that statement. After all, you cannot be responsible for EVERYTHING that happens around you, can you? Well, according to the Law of Attraction, yes. And in that law, it also states that there is NO assertion, only attraction. Meaning, we cannot MAKE things happen, but rather we can only get into the alignment that matches the vibration that attracts a particular something. Knowing and subscribing to this universal law, provides you with great empowerment to "consciously calibrate" your state of being to align with who you are on a more frequent level.

So, this brings us to some lessons with exercises that will help you make your Personal Brand DNA more tangible by realizing all the ways you can express your attributes into your external environment. Let's dig in!

Lesson1: Applying Your Personal Brand Through the Senses

"All credibility, all good conscience, all evidence of truth come only from the senses."

-Friedrich Nietzsche

How conscious are you about your sensory capabilities? It's time to gain a new appreciation of our abilities to take in the information around you, process it, and respond to it. Understanding the impact of this human gift is imperative to leveraging your Personal Brand Presence DNA to become the best version of yourself.

Every one of us are inundated with sensory stimulation throughout our days. Some of us have to consciously manage the frequent feeling of that stimulation overload with all the sounds, the visuals, the smells, the tastes, and other elements. So how do we choose what to pay attention to? Which ones to ignore?

Coming from a fascinating study in the book *Brand Sense* by Martin Lindstrom, we now know the extent to which we and our audiences use our senses to collect and analyze their information in the decision-making process.

Lindstrom reports in his research that there is a real correlation between activating sensory memories, be it sound, visual, smell or tactile, and the increase in the bond you can create with them with your audience. He states, "*The more sensory memory is activated, the greater the bond is to the Brand.*"

Think about what you wear, your tone, and speed of your voice, and whether you shake hands or hug someone upon meeting them. Do you make solid eye contact with others? Each of these actions adds to the multisensorial experience. With that increased information, broader perceptions are formed about your Brand in others' minds faster than without a multi-sensory input.

This is exactly where you can begin taking control of, managing, and elevating the perceptions others have of you. Let's take this a little deeper.

Take, for instance, your sense of sight. Have you thought of how your Personal Brand is experienced visually? Do you "show up" in alignment with your Personal Brand Style?

"83% of the information we retain is received visually!"

– Martin Lindstrom, *Brand Sense*

Martin Lindstrom expresses, "*Sight is the most seductive of all the senses. It often overrules the others and has the power to persuade us against all logic.*" Humans are constantly making decisions or judgment calls based on what they believe they see.

Here's a question—How is your Brand VISUALLY congruent with your Brand's style attributes? What about your differentiators and even your Brand promise? If your Brand attribute listed the style "polished," are you showing up that way? Are you dressing polished? Are you articulating thoughts and ideas in a polished way? Are your actions, behaviors, and gestures appropriately polished for the environment you are in?

These are the things you need to start challenging yourself with according to your own Personal Brand Presence DNA attributes. You're basically opening Pandora's Box with this kind of clarity, as more and more questions arise.

Remember the section on cognitive dissonance versus resonance? The senses are a primary area to focus on when you want to manage the level of cognitive resonance, and decrease the cognitive dissonance others may develop of your Personal Brand.

As a business owner, you are responsible for how the business is marketed from a visual perspective. Start thinking of how else you can leverage how your Personal Brand's attributes are affirmed within your physical environment, the look and feel of your brochures and website. It's a lot to think about, and this is just one of the six senses.

It's time to act and implement all the attributes that make your Personal Brand Presence DNA so special. This will be the key to your transformation to what makes you—you. Embrace this process, realizing that it will be done in small baby steps. Test things out, learn as you go. See how the environment you live and work in truly fits who you've identified and defined in your DNA.

I'll now be introducing a series of exercises that will build on the DNA foundation you have already created throughout all the exercises so far in this book. The following exercises are designed to get you thinking and acting more "on-Brand."

Don't rush. Take your time to walk through and grow with each new learning opportunity and task to become more conscious, strategic, and deliberate in shaping how your Personal Brand DNA gets showcased in the world around you.

Let's do some work on the senses. Going beyond sight, let's realize there is a stream of continuous perceptions being picked up on, assessed, and categorized by whomever is in your experience at every moment. Don't disregard what is actually happening when someone is hearing you speak about something. Consider your tone of voice, the pace with which you speak, and the volume and amount of speaking you do.

I had a client who, when we first met, spoke with extreme speed. I could tell she was a very type-A personality, and there was no doubt that she was highly energetic and passionate about life and what she does for a living. But within 10 minutes of our conversation, I was exhausted keeping up with her run-on conversation. I wanted to tell her to stop and take a breath! Her pace was confronting my natural pace and it made me uncomfortable. I took the time to gently coach her about this perception and she acknowledged her energy and noted that she gets nervous and excited when meeting new people.

When we started digging into identifying and defining her Personal Brand Attributes, she naturally became more confident and assured of her own way of being and started relaxing into her truth which introduced a new pace to her presence. Her slower pace enabled others to connect with her in a gentler way with ease and flow. It was also a much more authentic way of being for her. And she began enjoying meeting new prospects and sharing her skills and story.

LET'S RECAP!

All of our Personal Brand Attributes are perceived, judged, and catalogued away in just an instant, creating impressions and perceptions you may or may not have chosen. When you greet someone, is it with a firmly engaging handshake? Or do you keep your distance or maybe you give a quick hug-like gesture? Whatever you choose, your counterpart is picking up on and building perceptions— good, bad, or indifferent.

Let's now find out what flushes out for you by completing a **Personal Brand Multisensory Activity**, a **Visual Identity Assessment**, and answer some powerful reflective questions.

These activities are designed to get your Personal Brand more tangible through working on a more holistic, rightside of the brain, creative way. It will help you start to manage the Gestalt of how your Personal Brand is perceived with resonance.

Remember when we talked about you ALREADY having a Personal Brand near the beginning of this book and that the real question to ask was "Are you in control of it?" It is time to take control. These next three exercises will all help clarify and lead the way to building how your Brand is experienced in a natural, aligned way.

1. See Brand Exercise Ch 7/1, Page 165 – Applying & Enhancing Your Personal Brand Through the Senses.
2. See Brand Exercise Ch7/2, Page 167 – Visual Identity Assessment Checklist.
3. See Brand Exercise Ch7/3, Page 168 - Reflective Questions for Actioning.

Lesson 2: Assess & Align Your Behaviors to Your Values and Style Attributes

You now have the opportunity to assess and align your behaviors with your values and style attributes in a variety of creative ways. The next three exercises in this lesson help to uncover gaps and align all the facets of your life to a new awareness of your Personal Brand Presence DNA.

Ask yourself—How "on-brand" are you right now? Are you showing up according to how you have defined your values and style attributes? Oftentimes, when we define our unique Personal Brand Presence DNA, we establish some of them out of desire to be more of them. Because we aren't quite 100% there yet. I call this setting a "future present state." This happens when you know something is a core attribute that you want to become more of, but because of your past, mostly external environments, it has kept you from feeling the freedom to do so. Now is the time to recognize those "gaps" and start realizing new behaviors, and set goals and intentions, that affirm your DNA attributes on a regular basis.

This exercise will help you evaluate your current behaviors against your attribute definitions and where you may fall short, right now, and offer opportunities and actions to improve the alignment over time to become more and more "on-brand."

Contemplate the areas of this low-hanging fruit and identify some quick wins where you can begin raising a particular value or Brand Style attribute one day, or one week, at a time.

These exercises are helping you design your environment to have more control over how your Personal Brand is perceived and in alignment. They are powerful tools that can, even with subtle, conscious changes, transform your world.

Trust the process.

You'll be asked to rate how you are currently behaving according to your DNA to get more clarity on areas you are and could be better at being more "on-brand." Have fun with this, get intentional about it and love that you are getting closer and closer to full alignment!

*[See Brand Exercise Ch 7/4, Page 169
– Be "On-Brand" - Rate & Action Your Attributes.]*

Your Words have Power.

There is an extremely powerful concept regarding the vocabulary we use every day. It can be highly generative or contractive. Because words have emotions attached to them. Especially in specific contexts in our lives. Being mindful of the thoughts we think, the words we use, and the emotions behind them can reveal a lot about what we continue to manifest in our experiences every day. Have you ever thought about that?

"I must watch the words I use, because they create the world I see."

-Karen Solmansohn

Up-Level Your Experiences Through Your Own Personal Brand Vocabulary

Our words build our worlds. Becoming conscious about your words and what you are generating with them is imperative to managing the perceptions you want others to have of your Personal Brand. What could change for you when you know that your vocabulary sets the tone for your future, what you begin to manifest, and the relationships you attract and endure?

Our vocabulary sets the TONE for our future to build, or destroy, expand, or contract a situation, heal or hurt, attract, or repel. Knowing this can stop you in your tracks. Hearing yourself talk at a newly conscious level can create unique visceral experiences that enable you to feel a transformation happening in the moment.

Your next assignment guides you in mapping out powerful, generative words that will help to create the construct of a new narrative toward speaking/thinking more in alignment with your Personal Brand Presence DNA.

As you walk through the Brand vocabulary exercise, make sure you are not just looking through a thesaurus for your additional words, but rather think through how you will action your attributes and how you define each of them. See what other words pop into your mind that relate to that attribute. Embrace it by adding it to your list.

These words should become part of you.

So, utilize your new Personal Brand vocabulary...your distinctive "brand-speak" with:

- Everyday conversations
- Business and personal letters
  - Emails
  - Your "Brand Identity Statement" (30 second commercial)
  - Promotional pieces/social media/etc.
  - Infuse into your website content, especially your "About Me" page
  - On-hold messages
  - Initial client intake discussions
  - Sales presentations
  - Thank-you cards
  - Family and friends conversations

Go ahead, dive into this exercise now and enjoy the creative flow that arises from what you know to be true about your Brand-speak. After you complete this, start using the vocabulary regularly and notice what shifts in your world.

[See Brand Exercise Ch7/5, Page 172
– Building Your Personal Brand Vocabulary.]

Lesson 3: Closing Your Personal Brand Gaps

There is so much more you can do to fill out "holes" in your Personal Brand information. So, don't get overwhelmed and feel that all this has to happen right now. It doesn't. Remember that this is a process and it will only do good when you can feel totally present for the next steps to take place.

This section is here to remind you to finish what you've started regarding the activities in this book. By themselves, these activities stirred up lots of thought, consciousness, and inspiration to help you grow into being more generative within your Personal Brand Presence. But, it doesn't stop there. Taking action on what you've created will catapult you into alignment that much faster. Are you ready?

Personal branding is a never-ending process of reaffirming who you are and stepping into it in tangible, and thoughtful ways. The beauty of it all is that you are now clearer than ever before to stay in your lane and continue to evolve more and more into your authentic self.

You are the one in charge. Let's remember to close the gaps incrementally as you are getting more and more conscious and aligned with who you are.

Carve out 30 minutes now to review your Personal Brand Presence exercises and fill in the blanks, add to your outputs, dot your "i's" and cross your "t's" so to speak so you can feel complete.

ACTION: Make Your Standards of Living More Tangible

1. Take a moment to review your Standards of Living that you mapped out in Chapter 4. Each of these areas are building blocks for you to tackle once a month or once a quarter until you have mastered them. Be sure you have listed the supportive action steps in each Standards of Living area with distinctive timelines and details, just as you would in goal setting.

2. Take the next step and put some of those supportive actions onto a calendar and set some timeline goals when applicable to begin getting some quick wins and build momentum in the changing of your environment. As you evolve and grow so, too, will your Standards of Living. Make sure that you check in with them every six months or so, updating them and adjusting them to better suit you in living your Brand.

In the next action your imagination and creativity can blossom even more.

ACTION: Infuse Your Environment with Multisensory On-Brand Elements

Review the work you did with the Personal Brand Multisensory activity and start taking action on up leveling the resonance of your Brand Attributes. What does your Brand LOOK like? Where in your current office and/or home can you "pepper in" some of this description you filled out in the activity? Or what other sensory area is needing a bit of revival and "on-brand" focus? (i.e. if RED is your "Personal Brand color" then assess what clothes in your closet are red and decide if you need a new red dress, or tie!)

Is there a wall you can paint a certain color in your home or office? What music/genre playlist can you create and play in your office or home that resonates with you? These ideas could be endless and now is the time to make your outputs form the exercise start to come alive!

Exercise 6: (BONUS!) Marketing Smarter, Not Harder!

Before you spend one more dollar in marketing and advertising, read through this checklist and ensure your communication is as powerful and on-brand as possible! This handy checklist will help you become more intentional about the information you disseminate to your audiences and begin to be more consistent in your tone, messaging, and visual identity. Use this checklist to assess every piece of advertising you disseminate to your market.

Take a minute to review all 19 questions and make it a practice to do so with each marketing campaign or message you decide to create.

[See BONUS Brand Exercise Ch7/6, Page 173
– Advertising Effectiveness Checkpoints.]

Leverage the results of your Personal Brand Assessment tool from Chapter 1.

In that exercise, you identified the low-hanging fruit areas that you can quickly build on and leverage in your everyday life. Now that you have your Brand Style and Values decided, what would you do differently to affirm these attributes in the areas you scored low on from the results of your assessment? Each of these areas are designed to help you get started on the fast-track of leveraging your Personal Brand Presence DNA.

Lesson 4: The Power of Affirmation

If you have done the work so far in this book and flushed out the attributes that make up who you are, you have already experienced the power of clarity you get from identifying and defining something important to you. I bet you have reminisced about your work, the words you selected, and your attribute definitions over and over throughout this process.

You've thought deeply about how your values and style attributes resonate with you at the core. And you've randomly noticed how these attributes are showing up in your everyday life as you acknowledge your thoughts, actions, and behaviors.

Yep, it happened to me too. I caught myself calibrating regularly to my Values and Style. And still to this day I am very aware of when I am out of alignment and need to recalibrate to get back into my Personal Brand lane! I love being so conscious of that now and having the ability to re-align quickly back to my state of ease and flow of alignment.

"All that we are is the result of all we have thought."

- Buddha

Just by thinking about the relationship between yourself and these words you've chosen, you have activated a vibrational coherence that begins the process of **self-efficacy**, our perceived ability to control moral outcomes and respond flexibly when our self-concept is questioned (*The Psychology of Change: Self-Affirmation and Social Psychological Intervention,* Cohen & Sherman, 2014).

This means you are *already* starting to "protect" and align with who you know yourself to be from the inside out...*Personal Brand Clarity.*

That is so cool. But this is the first step of the process of becoming your full potential. Alignment is your work now. Recognizing when you are in resonance and when you are in dissonance of your unique Personal Brand Presence will be key for you to generate the real magic within the power of intention and the ability to manifest more and more of the same resonance as you continue to elevate with confidence.

Affirmations are a tool to help you realign, stay in your lane, and up your vibration so that you can sustain the awareness of your best self. The following affirmations are generic for the Personal Brand Presence students of this process, but knowing what you know now, the words will have deeper meaning to them and still enable you to resonate with their power to shift you into alignment.

Now that we know more about the theories supporting positive affirmations, here are six examples of evidence from empirical studies that suggest that positive self-affirmation practices can be beneficial: *(compiled by Catherine Moore, Psychologist, MBA, author of the article*

"Positive Daily Affirmations: Is There Science Behind It?" at www.PostivePsychology.com)

1. Self-affirmations have been shown to decrease health-deteriorating (Sherman et al., 2009; Critcher & Dunning, 2015);
2. Self-affirmations have been used effectively in that led people to increase their physical behavior (Cooke et al., 2014).
3. They may help us to perceive otherwise "threatening" messages with less resistance, including interventions (Logel & Cohen, 2012).
4. They can make us less likely to dismiss harmful health messages, responding instead with the intention to change for the better (Harris et al., 2007) and to eat more fruit and vegetables (Epton & Harris, 2008).
5. They have been linked positively to academic achievement by mitigating GPA decline in students who feel left out at college (Layous et al., 2017).
6. Self-affirmation has been demonstrated to lower stress and rumination (Koole et al., 1999; Weisenfeld et al., 2001).

With all of this powerful evidence we have regarding the use of affirmations, I have composed a few specifically for the Solopreneur/Leader reading this book and dedicating themselves to their own self-efficacy and evolution.

I recommend saying the ***Affirmations/Personal Brand Declarations*** out loud every day, at least at first, until you get into a regular flow of self-awareness. Then, recite them weekly, and then as needed to help you get back to your full aligned self. We all fall out of alignment. That is just a process of expansion. Things come our way in life that cause us all to veer out of our lane now and then, but this contrast is the catalyst for expansion and once we are able to recognize that fact, we can allow ourselves to realign faster.

I wrote these for you (feel free to print this page!)

MY DAILY Personal Brand DECLARATIONS!

I consciously and continuously MANAGE my Personal Brand.

I am brilliant at building my strong Personal Brand to create the desired PERCEPTION in the mind of my audience.

I will NOT be a commodity in the minds of my audience, rather I will continuously create a MEMORABLE Personal Brand EXPERIENCE.

I will be RELEVANT to my audience by CONNECTING to the values and needs of others and being true to what I stand for.

I will be DISTINCTIVE to my audience by STANDING OUT UNIQUELY, decidedly different with PURPOSE, and being true to what I stand for.

I will be CONSISTENT to my audience by SHOWING UP the SAME WAY every time, walking the talk, and being true to what I stand for.

Living my Personal Brand is a CONSCIOUS, STRATEGIC and DELIBERATE process that I take seriously.

"I AM A Personal Brand MASTER!"

LET'S RECAP!

Remember your Personal Brand Presence is GENERATIVE...meaning that you are always expanding into becoming more and more of your unique Brand DNA, in ways that adjust to our ever-changing world around us. It is all a part of our own evolution. Embracing it is a valuable skill to have and will enable you to evolve faster and with more ease and flow.

Affirmations are tools. Tools to get you calibrated to who you know yourself to be. When you recite affirmations that resonate with you, your vibration rises and begins to support your positive intentions in miraculous ways. Affirmations are designed to help you care about how you feel and get there!

I trust your journey through this process has been creative, insightful, and even a little tough. Congratulations, and keep your clarity on track by reviewing your work often and reciting these affirmations regularly.

This book has provided you with the tools to uncover a Personal Brand built on YOUR authentic self! Keep this book accessible and commit to taking action on these exercises. You will become more conscious, strategic and deliberate with your Personal Brand Presence and begin attracting experienes that align with who you are! Buckle up!

"Strong, resilient
Personal Brands are:
Clear on their value position,
Confident in their promise,
& Consistent in their delivery."

-Suzanne Tulien,
Brand Clarity Expert,
Brand Ascension

———

CONCLUSION

Well, I see you've got Personal Brand Presence! Do you FEEL it? I'm talking about YOU, and what's now become conscious from deep inside your Personal Brand's DNA!!

Humans are complex constructs of amazing thoughts, actions, philosophies, and ways of being. So, this journey you decided to take for yourself had to get to the core of who you are and what you continue to become more of. With clarity and focus, you can now move into being more and more of who you know yourself to be.

More *internally driven*, and less *externally impacted*.

In my formative years, as I mentioned in the opening of this book, I had such a desire to "fit in" and become a master chameleon in order to be "seen." As I look back on that part of my life, I realize how exhausting it really was. Being bullied kept me trapped in fear. I so longed to become independent of what others' thought of me (but didn't know how or what I needed to do to get there).

Back to my story from the introduction...fast forward into my professional world...

I started working early, when my dad would get me summer lawn mowing jobs, and a few babysitting gigs to start putting cash in my bank account (to buy my own car at 16!). Those were jobs I didn't really get to choose. But when I got old enough to choose what I wanted to do, I was attracted to the graphic design industry. My brother had exposed me to that opportunity as he went off to college to study graphic design and I became intrigued. I liked the idea because I was already a very visual person. Hence, I was a strong visual learner and was fascinated by the function that design played in our psyche —manipulating our behaviors, choices, and our emotions.

I landed jobs in magazine publishing, public relations, print, marketing/advertising, and graphic design industries through my college years and beyond. I became president of a local advertising federation and was deeply entrenched in the external strategic efforts of the function of marketing for business growth. Falling into a position of Creative Projects Manager for an advertising company for two years, we grew through acquisition of thirteen other brands. There I began understanding the origination of internal Brand strategy. It begins from the inside out. It was time to start my own design boutique called I.D. By Design, focusing on corporate identity design (logos) and collateral pieces (back to the external focus of marketing). It was then, while owning my own company, where I had a major BFO ("blinding flash of the obvious") which led me to begin the journey toward my Brand consulting passion.

What was the BFO that I had? After experiencing reaction after reaction of my business owner clients realizing the "upgrade'of their visual Brand identity look and feel, and admitting to their lack of "readiness" to step into what that new look and feel was representing, I knew I had to switch gears in what I was offering them.

You see, a new logo design is not a new Brand.

And more importantly, it will not change the current situation of your business. A new logo design minus the identifying, defining and aligning to what your company stands for, is just "lipstick on the pig." Fresh paint on the same ol' operation, so to speak. That was my **BFO** and I didn't like what I realized I was doing for my clients, even though the designs were greatly appreciated and boasted upon by my clients. They had no idea what I realized, because they believed what so many business owners believe; that their logo is their Brand.

My realization pivoted me to abruptly cease my design services temporarily, and commit to helping the client clarify what their Brand actually stood for. Identifying, defining, and then aligning to their own value position, create consistencies that build trust, and be utterly dedicated to deliver on their own Brand promise. That is the fundamental construct that causes businesses to expand exponentially.

So, I invented it. Hence, Brand Ascension consulting and training was born (2004).

I can certainly say that doing this work for myself, yes, I practice what I preach, has been the catalyst of my passion for building self-aligned Brands. Over the years, I have experienced my own stretches in growth, stepping out of my comfort zones, and realizing my own power within.

I will now share with you my Personal Brand WHY STATEMENT:

"I exist to be a cocreative partner in the evolution of personal alignment and authenticity; catalyzing consciousness, inspiration, and growth."

Part of the generative evolution of my "why" has been made tangible in this book project, and my new online course for solo professionals. This is exactly what being generative with your Brand looks like. I am always asking myself "what is the next level I can evolve into within my Brand Values and Style Attributes? How can I express my Brand in even more tangible ways to fulfill my purposeful passion in every dimension of my life?"

From the work you did in this book, you are enabled to:

- Deepen your commitment to your Values.
- Get creative expressing more fully your Personal Brand Style (sight, sound, taste, touch, smell!).
- Stay confident knowing what continues to make you different.
- Align to your Personal Brand Standards of Living every day.

- Reign yourself back into your Personal Brand power with your new Mantra.
- Remember why you're here, in this body, and on this earth with your "Why" statement.

It's a deep concept, I know, but oh so nourishing for your soul, and for everyone who is in your path of life and business to experience about you! I am so excited and proud of your clarity and focus!

I want to congratulate you on taking this journey and self-authoring your future. In my opinion, not enough of us take the time to relish in this process and become more familiar with our own selves so that we can drive our experiences in ways we never thought we could before.

You have uncovered your *Personal Brand Clarity.*

You ARE in the driver's seat now. Clear, confident, consistent, and inspired to impact your world. You are discerning differently now than when you started. Trust that you are evolving more and more into your potential.

The world has been waiting...what's in store for you as you begin to become more authentic, consistent, and generative in your way of being?

What's next? You are learning to be you out in the world, showing your Personal Brand Presence to everyone you meet. Growing in your confidence that you, every day, as you are meant to be.

And know that The Universe has your back!

All is well.

Namaste.

"The only thing that
is meant to be
is your own expansion."

- Abraham Hicks

———————

BRAND EXERCISES
Chapter Location Reference

CHAPTER 6

CHAPTER 7

CHAPTER 1 | EXERCISE 1

Self-Actualization Assessment

RATE YOURSELF for LEVELS OF SELF ACTUALIZATION!
On a scale of 1-5, with 1 = 0% & 5 = 100%:
How would you rate yourself right now in showing up with this characteristic.

- **Acceptance and Realism**: have realistic perceptions of themselves, others, and the world around them.

- **Problem-centering**: are concerned with solving problems outside of themselves, including helping others and finding solutions to problems in the external world.

- **Spontaneity**: are spontaneous in their internal thoughts and outward behavior.

- **Autonomy and Solitude:** have a need for independence and privacy.

- **Continued Freshness of Appreciation:** tend to view the world with a continual sense of appreciation, wonder and awe.

- **Peak Experiences:** have what Maslow termed peak experiences, or moments of intense joy, wonder, awe, and ecstasy.

- **Enjoying the Journey:** while self-actualized people have concrete goals, they do not see things as simply a means to an end.

35 Maximum/Your Total: _____

ABRAHAM MASLOW, US Psychologist, known for the Hierarchy of Needs and work on Human desire for fulfillment.

"What a man can be, he must be. This need we may call self-actualization...It refers to the desire for self-fulfillment, namely, to the tendency for him to become actualized in what he is potentially.

It is the desire to become more and more what one is, to become everything that one is capable of becoming."
- Abraham Maslow

Maslow, A. H. (1943). A Theory of Human Motivation, Psychological Review 50, 370-96. Maslow, A.H. (1943). Motivation and personality. New York: Harper. Maslow, A. (1970). Motivation and personality (2nd ed.). New York: Harper & Row. 4 Wahba, M.A. & Bridwell, L.G. (1976). Maslow reconsidered: A review of research on the need hierarchy theory. Organizational Behavior and Human Performance , 15, 212–240.

Identify Your Personal Brand Values

When we are in alignment to what we stand for—we are perceived as more authentic and consistent. When we live by our values, we increase the reservoir of the "goodwill" and "intention" of our brand to our "audiences" in which we serve. **When we don't live by our values**, we lose good-will and erode relationships with others. Values are not behaviors in and of themselves, but rather a reflection of something we say we are and want to be.

Alignment to what your personal brand stands for occurs when your **values match the behaviors you act out**. We call this acting with "Cognitive Resonance." Often we espouse to certain values, but when the behaviors don't match, there is misalignment in the minds of your audiences, or what we call 'Cognitive Dissonance,' thus creating the potential for mistrust. (*The following is an exercise adapted from Tony Schwartz, author of The Power of Full Engagement.*)

1. List three qualities (adjectives) you **can't stand** when you see them or experience them in other people.

   _____   _____   _____

2. List three qualities (adjectives) you **are embarrassed about** when they surface in your own behaviors.

   _____   _____   _____

3. List three qualities (adjectives) you notice when you (your brand) are **performing at your very best.**

   _____   _____   _____

For questions **1** & **2** above, now (in the space below) list the **OPPOSITE** of the words you identified as these reflect the contrary to what you wrote and represent what you truly stand for.

Opposite to the above words from 1 & 2:

1. _____   _____   _____

2. _____   _____   _____

Now do the following:

1   Consolidate any words that overlap or are similar as reported in the opposite listings for 1 & 2 above and as originally identified in question 3 (all nine words); picking the top most resonating words and discarding the rest.

2   List the selected remaining words in the first column in the table below. In the second column, identify each by their level of importance to you on a scale of 1—10 with 1=Lowest and 10=Highest.

3   Then circle the top four based on their level of importance. Rating the level of importance is a "sanity check" to ensure if it will hold up to the test of what your personal brand stands for.

4   In the third column, rate how fully your brand lives each value currently (in both business and personal life) using the following scale of **1 = Rarely — 10 = Almost Always**

I Value... (in noun form)	Importance of Value- 1=Lowest; 10=Highest	How fully does your brand currently LIVE this value (1=Rarely - 10=Almost Always)

Finally, decide on your top 4 CORE VALUES and circle them from the previous chart.
Transfer those circled values onto your
Personal Brand Presence DNA template.
Downloadable .pdf -
https://bit.ly/2O2CBNW **or**
https://brandascension.com/wp-
content/uploads/2020/07/PersonalBRANDPresence-blnk-template.doc

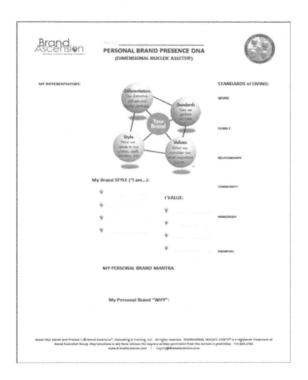

CONGRATULATIONS!

Take the time **to CELEBRATE** your completion of this exercise—
you are well on your way to elevating your clarity in your
PERSONAL brand!

Define Your Personal Brand Values

DEFINING YOUR VALUE ATTRIBUTES: This is one of the most important solidifying steps, because it brings the value to life so you can make it more tangible in your experience. Refer to examples in Chapter 1.

VALUE ("I Value...") : DEFINITION (How you show up everyday eliciting this value)

1. _____ : _____
   _____
   _____
   _____

2. _____ : _____
   _____
   _____
   _____

3. _____ : _____
   _____
   _____
   _____

4. _____ : _____

_____

_____

_____

4 VALUES IS OPTIMAL - But if there is a "must-have" value that you cannot live without, list it below.

5. _____ : _____

_____

_____

_____

These value definitions are YOURS - not from theWebsters Dictionary, but in your own words as to how YOU show up within these terms you chose. You are applying meaning to them based on how you lean into aligning with them every day in every way.
They should give you goose bumps when you read them, because they resonate so well with who you are.

Identify Your Personal Brand Style

Instructions: To begin to uncover your Personal Brand style attributes (the manner in which you want to present yourself to others) let's step outside of the box and get you thinking creatively! This will move you to the right side of your brain. Answer the following questions as best you can with the first instincts you have about your brand style! Have fun with this!

Question	Specific Answer	List 3-4 Descriptive Adjectives	Choose the <u>ONE</u> word that most represents you.
EXAMPLE: If your brand were represented by a specific **SMELL,** what would it be?	**Peppermint**	**Exhilarating Refreshing Inspiring**	**Refreshing**
If your brand were a specific make & model of a **CAR,** what would it be? (Toyota Tacoma, Kia Optima, Tesla X, etc.)			
If your brand were represented by a **GENRE of MUSIC,** what would it be? (jazz, country, pop, classical, rap, alternative, etc.)			
If your brand were a **LINE of CLOTHING,** what best represents you? (i.e., The Gap, Levi's, Chanel, Under Armour.)			

Question	Specific Answer	List 3-4 Descriptive Adjectives	Choose the <u>ONE</u> word that most represents you.
If your brand were an **ANIMAL**, what best represents you? (i.e., Eagle, Panther, Dog, Gerbil, Kangaroo, etc.)			
If your brand were represented by **COLOR**, what best represents you? (Deep blue, burgundy, orange, violet, butter yellow, etc)			
If your brand were a **DESSERT**, what best represents you? (i.e., Cherry Ice Cream, Brownie Sunday, Blueberry Pie, etc.)			

Are you are a bit surprised by these outcomes?

Personal Brand Style continues...
Now do the following...

- Pull all the final (right column adjectives) words from exercise into the first column in the table below.
- In the second column, identify their level of importance on a scale of 1—10 with 1 = Lowest & 10 = Highest.
- Circle the top four, based on their level of importance. Rating the level of importance is a "sanity check" to ensure if it will hold up to the test of how your brand shows up.

139

- In the third column, rate how fully your Personal Brand currently lives each style (through your business & personal life).
- Finally, agree on your top 4 STYLE attributes and circle them. Transfer those circled Style words onto your Personal Brand Presence DNA Onesheet.

"I am.." (in adjective form)	Importance of Style to YOU! 1=Lowest; 10=Highest	How fully does your brand currently LIVE this Style (1=Rarely - 10=Always)

...Now it is time to Define Your Brand Style!

Define Your Brand Style!

From the previous page, list your top four [or five] circled Style attributes and define them here. In your definition, express how you show up expressing this attribute in your everyday life.

DEFINING YOUR STYLE ATTRIBUTES

STYLE ("I am...."): DEFINE (How do you show up eliciting this style in your every life.)

1. _____: _____
   _____
   _____
   _____

2. _____: _____
   _____
   _____
   _____

3. _____: _____
   _____
   _____
   _____

4. _____: _____
   _____
   _____
   _____

4 STYLE ATTRIBITES ARE OPTIMAL! - But if there is a "must-have" style that you cannot live without, list it below.

5. _____ : _____

_____

_____

_____

Remember, these definitions describe "How" you show up in each of these areas every day. Take a look again at the Brand Style samples provided by graduates of this program in this book so you can get a sense of what your definitions should be showcasing about how you "ARE" representative of these attributes.

Once you've written the first draft for each. Put them away for a day or two and then come back to them and edit/add more depth as you have had the time to ponder them a bit, and refer to them in your daily experiences.

Identify & Define Your Unique Differentiators

These skill sets and quality attributes distinguish you from everyone else. They can include your unique approach to servicing your clients (if you are a solo-preneur, or professional in the work place) to your accomplishments throughout your life (e.g. writing a book, painting masterpieces, unique hobbies and certifications, non-profit board positions, volunteer work/awards, other skill sets, etc.). It also could include your unique mix/blend of talent such as your degrees, certifications, years of experience, vastness of experience, awards, etc. Think of all the core assets your personal brand has to bring to the "credential" table and to exemplify your brand.

Consider the following dimensions when identifying your unique PERSONAL BRAND DIFFERENTIATORS: It is NOT expected for you to have a differentiator in each of these areas. These are just areas of dimension that help to trigger "aha's" that may not have been thought of before. Try to uncover at least 5 key differentiators for yourself and quantify them if you can. (Quantifying simply means to include a number or statistic to the differentiator, such as "Author of three books," "twenty-eight years in the industry," "First prize in Chili cook-off four yrs in a row," "Speak three languages," "Play two instruments," etc.).

1. **AUTHORSHIP:** Have you written a book? Poems? Recipe books? Illustrated a child's book? Written course manuals? Defined a process? Scored music? Invented a game?

2. **VOLUNTEERISM:** Are you engaged in volunteer work? If so, what do you do? How many years? What specific things have you accomplished you are proud of as part of the volunteer group?

3. **UNIQUE HOBBIES/SKILLS:** Do you engage in a unique hobby or craft that helps to express your brand style and values? Do you sell your crafts?

4. **EXPERTISE**: Are you an expert in something? Building planes, cars, or doll houses? What skills qualify you as an expert in your job?

5. **DISTINCTIVE OR ONE-OF-A-KIND SKILL SETS:** Think about your quality attributes, credentials, skill sets, that distinguishes you from all others in your industry category, that no one else can lay claim to exactly like you. This could include talents, like playing instruments, singing, dancing, painting, photography, etc.

6. **PROPRIETARY INTELLECTUAL CAPITAL:** Are you an inventor? What do you exclusively possess and how do you leverage—technology, trade secrets/patents, processes, methods, products, people (certifications, talent, knowledge, etc.)?

7. **DEGREES/CERTIFICATIONS:** Do you hold scholarly degrees, or certifications that raise your credentials beyond that of others?

8. **UNIQUE BEHAVIORAL ACTIONS:** (mostly for solo-preneurs) Do you consistently demonstrate unique customer service behaviors that are unique in your industry, and create a differentiated customer experience and set you apart from your competition.

9. **UNIQUE HERITAGE/HISTORY:** Do you have a unique lineage or heritage or "way of being" (Native Indian, Amish, German, Japanese, etc.) or have you followed in your ancestors' footsteps in the industry or business you run/work at?

10. **REACH or EXCLUSIVITY:** Do you have a unique breadth of clientele (e.g., customer base representative of 30 countries)? Or are you highly exclusive in your clientele profile?

11. **AWARDS:** What awards have you and/or your business won that makes you stand out?

12. **ASSOCIATION:** Is your personal brand associated with any organization outside your industry that creates a sense of greater belonging (e.g., American Heart Association, Breast Cancer, St. Jude's, Environmental Causes, Wildlife Conservation, etc.)?

FINAL DRAFT OF SELECTED DIFFERENTIATORS: List your differentiator, then describe it more clearly in the "Supportive Details" section. Try to include the quantifier in the "My Differentiator" section; i.e. "Four Industry Achievement Awards", then list in "Supportive Details" the types of awards received.

My Differentiator: **Supportive Details:**

1). _____: _____

_____

_____

_____

2). _____: _____

_____

_____

_____

3). _____: _____

_____

_____

_____

4). _____: _____

_____

_____

_____

5). _____: _____
_____
_____
_____

6). _____: _____
_____
_____
_____

7). _____: _____
_____
_____
_____

8). _____: _____
_____
_____
_____

9). _____: _____
_____
_____
_____

Got more? Feel free to add to this list on separate sheet of paper.

CHAPTER 4 | EXERCISE 1A

Work Standards of Living

WORK/PROFESSIONAL: State your over arching Standard of Living belief statement in the area of your work/professional life. *See example on next page—follow for all Standards.*

_____

_____

_____

_____

_____

List your **Values/Styles** that this statement supports:

_____

Supportive Actions: *(What are the first steps I need to begin to take to ensure I can live this Standard, and by when?)*

- _____

- _____

- _____

- _____

STANDARDS OF LIVING EXAMPLE:

This example showcases what this exercise is requesting from you. A Standards of Living statement will focus on each area on the six areas that make up your life surroundings and should illustrate your Personal Brand's overall level of expectation you commit to live up to. Notice how the "SUPPORTIVE ACTIONS" are fleshed out of their Standards of Living statement by breaking down the elements of the statement into actionable steps. Your "SUPPORTIVE ACTIONS" are designed to itemize actions and behaviors that will support and affirm the Standard you compose for each area (i.e. "What is the first thing you need to start doing to ensure this Standard of Living is followed?, then what is the next and next steps?")

CLIENT: Real Estate Agent (solo-professional)

WORK: I endeavor to receive **100% satisfaction** of my service, **celebrate successes,** and stay **up-to-date** on the latest products and programs, and contribute a percentage of my profits to a local **non-profit** that **supports my value** system.

Personal Brand Values/Style this Statement Supports:
Genuine, Compassionate, Gracious

Supportive Actions:

- Create and disseminate **customer feedback survey** after every client project, **by next month.**

- Seek out and attend **webinars/seminars, and conferences** that provide latest in technology and industry information at least **once a quarter.**

- Plan and host **a customer appreciation party** to celebrate successes with my clients by first month of **next quarter.**

- Identify local, values-based **nonprofit to submit contributions.** Identify percentage of profits within my financial model to contribute within the **next 30 days.**

CHAPTER 4 | EXERCISE 1B

Family Standards of Living

FAMILY (immediate): State your over arching Standard of Living belief statement in the area of your work/professional life. *See example on next page—follow for all Standards.*

_____

_____

_____

_____

_____

List your **Values/Styles** that this statement supports:

_____

Supportive Actions: *(What are the first steps I need to begin to take to ensure I can live this Standard, and by when?)*

- _____

- _____

- _____

- _____

CHAPTER 4 | EXERCISE 1C

Relationship Standards of Living

RELATIONSHIPS (friends/community/colleagues):

State your over arching Standard of Living belief statement in the area of your work/professional life. *See example on next page—follow for all Standards.*

_____

_____

_____

_____

_____

List your **Values/Styles** that this statement supports:

_____

Supportive Actions: *(What are the first steps I need to begin to take to ensure I can live this Standard, and by when?)*

- _____

- _____

- _____

- _____

CHAPTER 4 | EXERCISE 1D

Community Standards of Living

COMMUNITY (church, associations, voluneering, etc.): State your over arching Standard of Living belief statement in the area of your work/professional life. *See example on next page—follow for all Standards.*

_____

_____

_____

_____

_____

List your **Values/Styles** that this statement supports:

_____

Supportive Actions: *(What are the first steps I need to begin to take to ensure I can live this Standard, and by when?)*

- _____

- _____

- _____

- _____

CHAPTER 4 | EXERCISE 1E

Mind-Body
Standards of Living

MIND-BODY (self-care/growth): State your over arching Standard of Living belief statement in the area of your work/professional life. *See example on next page—follow for all Standards.*

_____

_____

_____

_____

_____

List your **Values/Styles** that this statement supports:

_____

Supportive Actions: *(What are the first steps I need to begin to take to ensure I can live this Standard, and by when?)*

- _____

- _____

- _____

- _____

CHAPTER 4 | EXERCISE 1F

Financial Standards of Living

FINANCIAL (your money habits/beliefs): State your over arching Standard of Living belief statement in the area of your work/professional life. *See example on next page—follow for all Standards.*

_____

_____

_____

_____

_____

List your **Values/Styles** that this statement supports:

_____

Supportive Actions: *(What are the first steps I need to begin to take to ensure I can live this Standard, and by when?)*

- _____

- _____

- _____

- _____

Crafting Your Personal Brand Mantra

To identify your Personal Brand Platform, review your list of brand style, and values attributes, and decide which of these you are most passionate about, have the most energy around, and have the courage to consistently and distinctively express all the time.

- Generally three to four words/attributes—and comes from the most dominant characteristics of your style, and/or values...the attributes of which permeates every thing else in your DNA.
- It exemplifies the most dominant characteristics of your Personal Brand DNA.
- Your mantra depicts what "you stand for," it encompasses the essence of your behavior and intention and is used as a personal "cheer" to refocus yourself on the power of your Personal Brand.

PERSONAL BRAND MANTRA SAMPLES:

TONYA:	**ASTUTE. AUTHENTIC. ANSWERABLE.**
CHEVY:	**L.I.F.E. = LEADERSHIP. INTEGRITY. FUN. EXCELLENCE!**
ANEISSA:	**GUARDIAN WITH GRACE**
STEPH:	**FUN. FOCUSED. RELATIONAL. REVOLUTIONARY!**
JON:	**S.A.I.L. = SINCERE. AUTHENTIC. INVENTIVE. LAUGH!**
STEVE:	**A^4 = AWARENESS. AUTHENTICITY. ACTION. ABUNDANCE.**
SARAH:	**S.A.G.E. = SASSY. A GENUINE EGALITARIAN.**

First, list any FOUR key attributes (values & style) from your Personal Brand Presence DNA:

_____   _____   _____   _____

Work with these words to begin to form a meaningful, **memorable phrase, or an acronym, or use them each as their own statement**. Use the space below to write out your thoughts & ideas. You can add additional words outside of your DNA—but very minimally. Remember, this is a highly personal statement that should resonate with you (it is NOT a tagline or catch phrase for your audience to resonate with), and should trigger in your mind the full essence of your Personal Brand Presence and motivate you towards alignment and "on-brand" actions and behaviors.

Mantra draft ideas:

1. _____

2. _____

3. _____

Final Mantra Choice:
(Must energize you and resonate at a deep level.)

_____

CHAPTER 5 | EXERCISE 2

Uncovering Your "Why"

Your Personal Brand's "WHY" is a concise statement or description of the core understanding of your true reason for being (PURPOSE) through championing your unique DNA attributes. The fundamentals of creating the your Brand's Why declaration includes answering the following questions to assist in a deeper dive into your way of being:

1. **"If I wasn't afraid and knew I couldn't fail, who would I be and what would I be doing?"**

    _____

    _____

    _____

2. **"What lights me on fire, gives me goose bumps, and makes my heart smile?"**

    _____

    _____

    _____

3. **"To truly live my WHY, what are the thoughts I think, the words I speak and the actions I take?"**

    Thoughts:_____

    _____

    Words: _____

    Actions:_____

4. **How do/will my Style and Value attributes align with my (WHY) reason for being?**

   _____

   _____

   _____

5. **What are three to four of my greatest strengths and natural abilities that show up when I am feeling my best, most authentic self, effortlessly?**

   1. _____

   2. _____

   3. _____

   4. _____

Now, reflect on these answers before moving into the next activity where you will craft your Personal Brand "Why" statement. These questions were designed to get you thinking deeper.

CHAPTER 5 | EXERCISE 3

Crafting Your Personal Brand "Why" Statement

Review your answers to the questions on the previous page. Now, **highlight or circle** the words and phrases that resonate most with you. Using those words and phrases, compose your first draft of your Brand's "WHY" statement below. Then **take an hour or two to contemplate** your first draft by memorizing it and repeating it in your head and out loud several times. Give it time to gel.

Return to your draft after a few hours (or the next day) and:

- **Revise and refine** to better clarify how to articulate your "WHY" more accurately, ensuring it fully resonates with your way of being in a fully self-actualized.

- Consider inserting some of your **VALUE and STYLE** attribute terms within the composition.

- Consider weaving in the essence of your **mantra.**

- **Brevity is powerful.** Edit and drill down to the most impactful vocabulary, eliminate the "fluff" and be as succinct as possible is as few words as possible. But remember your words create your world!

- *The final version should give you goose bumps when you read it!*

- Review some **examples** on the following page after this exercise.

My Brand's "WHY" - Draft #1

I exist to:

_____

_____

_____

_____

_____.

My Brand's "WHY" - Draft #2

I exist to:

_____

_____

_____

_____

My Brand's "WHY" - FINAL (goose bumps version!)

I exist to:

_____

_____

_____

_____

Personal Brand "WHY" Declaration Examples:

"I exist to create innovative, inspiring, and memorable environments that empower and perpetuate thoughtful, values-based leadership to evolve and elevate the lives of others."

. . . .

"I exist to give kindness and compassion to people I meet, bring joy to the lives of those I love; and encourage, support, and advocate for those I serve."

. . . .

"I exist to be coherent, deliver competence, and be strategically driven to leadership that produces game-changing results within lives I touch in an elegant fashion."

. . . .

"I exist to set people on fire through my free spirit so life force and human consciousness merge to create from abundance in manifold ways."

. . . .

"I exist to inspire higher levels of thinking while being patient and nurturing to encourage empowerment and confidence in those who experience me."

. . . .

"I exist to create an abundant life for myself, and use this abundance to support my family, friends, and community in creating and living the life they really want. I will make the rest of life the best of life."

160

CHAPTER 6 | EXERCISE 1

Personal Brand Authenticity Audit

Authenticity is a VIBRATION. YOU can feel it within you. People can feel it from you. But being authentic comes from the ability to thoroughly KNOW who you are at the core, and aligning to that so well that it becomes your nature. The following questions are designed as a self-assessment to help you determine the "elevation" to which your Personal Brand has reached your authentic alignment. Be honest in your answers to get a true assessment of what are the low-hanging fruit area to pay more attention to.

Each question has the following choices: 1=Never, 2, 3, 4, 5=Always

1. I always stand up for what I believe. _____
2. I fully live in accordance to my core values & beliefs. _____
3. I am the same person at work as I am at home. _____
4. I am passionate about my career as it leverages my true skills. _____
5. I am satisfied with my life, & enjoy seeking ways to enhance it. _____
6. I go after doing what I want to do without fear. _____
7. I am fulfilled in my romantic relationships. _____
8. I am in sync with the REAL me and am empowered to be me. _____
9. I don't hide how I truly feel. _____
10. I don't fret that everyone is happy before I can be. _____
11. I consciously dress the part of my brand. _____
12. I don't worry about what I should say in certain situations. _____
13. I schedule self-care regularly without guilt. _____
14. I am not easily influenced or manipulated by others. _____
15. I don't get intimidated by others. _____
16. I consciously assess my alignment when making choices. _____
17. I am comfortable maintaining my true self in situations. _____

Based on the rating assigned, add each of the ratings.   **TOTAL:** _____

Score of 70—85: Lots of strength to capitalize on; you have the Personal Brand characteristics of an inspiring leader, friend, confidant!

Score of 55—69: Keep up the self-development dive! With targeted & committed clarity & actions, you will elevate to your next level!

Score of less than 54: Lots of opportunity for improvement; with diligent and careful effort towards clarifying your Personal Brand Presence DNA attributes, you could begin elevating to more confidence and internal power to manifest & live your potential!

Personal Brand Consistency Audit

Consistency builds TRUST. And one of the most powerful contributors of a successful brand is its ability to create and follow consistent ways of being to ensure the desired perception of the experience (for all stakeholders) is delivered. The following questions are designed as a self-assessment to help you determine the "elevation" to which your brand has reached in differentiating itself consistently. Behaviors that are consistent with what your brand stands for are key factors in creating competitive advantage.

Rate each question: 1=Never, 2=Sometimes, 3=Often, 4=Always

1   I consistently behave in ways that reflect my values & style.   _____

2   I ensure my partners & vendors are "on-brand" with mine.   _____

3   I have a clear brand promise my customers expeerience consistently.   _____

4   My business visual identity is documented in a style guide for consistency._____

5   I use a unique brand vocabulary when representing what I do.   _____

6   I've established a consistent customer follow up protocol I follow.   _____

7   I ask for customer feedback relative to delivery of my brand promise.   _____

8   All my marketing is visually/consistently representative of my brand.   _____

9   My website "looks" like my brand & content is updated frequently.   _____

10 I fully understand the top 3 differentiators from my competition.   _____

11 When in business, I consciously dress the part of my brand.   _____

12 I regularly review my own processes to ensure I am living my brand.   _____

13 I consistently seek to learn new skills to enhance my expertise.   _____

14 I consistently go extraordinary lengths to "Wow" my customers.   _____

15 I get back to customers within 24 hours via phone, text, or email.   _____

16 I consciously assess my personal alignment when making choices.   _____

17 I support my community in areas that resonate with my brand values.   _____

Add each of the individual ratings to arrive at a total score.   TOTAL: _____

Score of 51—68: Strength to capitalize on; you have the behavioral dimension characteristics of a LEADING PRACTICE brand.

Score of 35—50: With targeted & committed improvement, behavioral dimension characteristics could be elevated to LEADING PRACTICE brand.

Score of less than 35: Lots of opportunity for improvement; with diligent and careful effort, behavioral dimension characteristics could be elevated to LEADING PRACTICE—start with low hanging fruit!

CHAPTER 6 | EXERCISE 3

How You Become More Authentic, Consistent & Generative

Knowing these characteristics are one thing, but applying them is another. Only you know where you need to work on leveraging these characteristics in your everyday life. And doing so will help you design the environments you need to live your potential!

This activity will kick-start you into thinking and acting more "on-brand." Take a look at the three areas below and identify at least one value and one style attribute that you can begin to work on to enhance the characteristic in your actions and behaviors. Making it real and relevant in your world will enable you to master it in real time.

For example:
ESSENTIAL CHARACTERISTIC = **CONSISTENT**
Personal Brand VALUE to apply: *"Environmental Stewardship"*
How will I apply:
"I will be more consistent in my efforts to recycle trash not only from our household but within my work environment. I will set up convenient systems to make it easier for me and my family to be more conscious and consistent in doing so. I will install low flow devices on my showers and toilets and be more mindful to turn off lights in areas of the house that are not being used."

ESSENTIAL CHARACTERISTIC = AUTHENTIC.

Personal Brand VALUE or STYLE to apply: _____.

How will I apply:

_____

_____

_____

ESSENTIAL CHARACTERISTIC = CONSISTENT.

Personal Brand VALUE or STYLE to apply: _____.

How will I apply:

_____

_____

_____

ESSENTIAL CHARACTERISTIC = GENERATIVE.

Personal Brand VALUE or STYLE to apply: _____.

How will I apply:

_____

_____

_____

Applying & Enhancing Your Personal Brand Through the Senses

Here's where you really begin to "show up" with your PERSONAL brand essence. You can change your environment to be more aligned with your personal brand by clarifying how it can be filtered and experienced through the six senses! This is a creative exercise that will get you thinking differently about how else you can present your brand at elevated levels. Think through and answer the questions below—I am sure your mind will be full of ideas!

- **SIGHT** - What does my PERSONAL brand **LOOK** like? Consider your physical attributes: how you look, dress, your brand colors, carry yourself with confidence, and how you present yourself to others—be descriptive!

  _____

  _____

  _____

- **SOUND** - What does my PERSONAL brand **SOUND** like? Consider your personal "brand speak" (vocabulary) distinctive tone or pitch, and pace. If your personal brand reflected a specific genre of music, what would that be? If your brand was represented by music, what would we hear?

  _____

  _____

  _____

- **SMELL** - What does my PERSONAL brand **SMELL** like? What particular scent resonates with you that you want others to associate with you. Do you have a preferred brand of cologne or perfume? _Smell is the most powerful mnemonic device (memory enhancing)_, so use this technique to build memorable experiences.

  _____

  _____

  _____

- **TASTE** - What does my PERSONAL brand **TASTE** like? Consider what tastes you want others to associate or experience with you. Are you tangy, or mellow, spicy or sweet? If your Brand had a flavor, what would it be?

  _____

  _____

  _____

- **FEEL** - How is my PERSONAL brand reflected through tactile **qualities**? Are you a hugger? Consider what textures of clothing represent you, how you shake hands, or shoulder pat...or do you high-five? Are you soft and comfy, or simple and structured?

  _____

  _____

  _____

- **INTUIT** - What does my brand "WHY" **EXPRESS INTUITIVELY?** (i.e., overall "take-away" impression.) Consider how your entire Personal Brand essence makes people _feel_ when they interact with you, as stated in your "WHY."

  _____

  _____

  _____

Get as creative as you can with these! This will help you craft new, uniquely "on-brand" customer experiences.
Feel free to use a separate sheet of paper
or compose in a word.doc.

Visual Identity Assessment Checklist

The following questions are designed as a self-assessment to help you determine the "elevation" to which your VISUAL BRAND IDENTITY (logo & collateral pieces, etc.) has reached in representing your unique business brand. The assessment is based on the three most powerful attributes of a successful brand: **Consistent, Relevant, and Distinctive. Answer YES or NO.**

1	My logo was professionally designed.	_____
2	My logo graphic is in several digital formats & resolutions.	_____
3	I know and understand the brand symbolism in my logo.	_____
4	My logo has a specific color scheme consistent in all marketing.	_____
5	My business cards are visually consistent with all marketing materials.	_____
6	I utilize both sides of my business cards to promote my brand.	_____
7	I know my logo's fonts and use them in all marketing materials.	_____
8	My visual brand is on every piece of collateral from my business.	_____
9	My logo design has a written brand narrative reflecting its meaning.	_____
10	My logo appears correctly & consistent on every marketing piece.	_____
11	My logo is designed to appear in both vertical & horzontal formats.	_____
12	My business design & name is legally trademarked/registered.	_____
13	I have a graphic standards guide representing my visual brand.	_____
14	My work environment reflects my visual brand identity.	_____
15	My customers can differentiate my visual brand from competitiors.	_____
16	My visual identity has remained consistent throughout life of business.	_____
17	My website URL & email address reflects my brand name.	_____
18	I use my logo on promotional items (mugs, pens, t-shirts, etc.)	_____
19	I own the specific digital fonts of my visual brand on my computer.	_____
20	I have a brand tagline that accompanies my logo presentation.	_____

Evaluating your score: Based on the rating assigned, score each item as follows: YES = 5, NO = 0

90 – 100 Very High Elevation: Strength to capitalize on; you have the visual brand identity characteristics of a LEADING PRACTICE brand.

80 – 89 High Elevation: Strength to build on; with a little improvement, visual brand identity characteristics could be elevated to LEADING PRACTICE brand.

70 – 79 Medium Elevation: With targeted and committed improvement, visual brand identity characteristics could be elevated to LEADING PRACTICE brand.

60 – 69 Low Elevation: Lots of opportunity for improvement; with diligent and careful effort, visual brand identity characteristics could be elevated to

LEADING PRACTICE—start with "low hanging fruit!"

CHAPTER 7 | EXERCISE 3

Reflective Questions for Actioning

Now that you have defined your Personal Brand Presence DNA (Dimensional Nucleic Assets®), ask yourself these questions:
(Answer swiftly and with confidence... you know this stuff!)

- How will I create the optimal Personal Brand experience for my audiences? (Family, friends, colleagues, community.)

  _____

  _____

- Will experiencing my Personal Brand be affirmed through the human senses: Sight, sound, scent, taste, and feel? Which ones, and how? (Complete multisensory exercise.)

- How will I keep my Brand Mantra top of mind?

  _____.

- How will my brand "WHY" guide my behavior?

  _____.

- Why will my audience want to be with me/include me often in everyday activities, meetings, events, and look forward to being with me again? _____.

- Does my Personal Brand reinforce something about who my friends are?

  _____.

- Where can I focus to find more opportunities to be fully generative?

  _____.

- Does my Personal Brand make people feel as though they are associating with something valuable and impactful? If so, how?

  _____

Be "On-Brand!" Rate & Action Your Attributes

Remember, building an authentic and successful brand is about consistently showing up the way you say you are—your unique Brand PRESENCE. There are two steps to this exercise. In Step 1, you will assess how consistent you are as brand in living your values and style attributes. In Step 2, you will identify those with biggest gaps in consistency and develop actions to address the gaps.

TIME TO ALLOT: 10 minutes for Step 1; 20 minutes for Step 2 (carve out some quality time on your calendar).

INSTRUCTIONS
STEP 1: When a you are in alignment to what you stand for—you show up more authentic and consistent. This alignment occurs when your values and style attributes are consistent with your behaviors. We refer to this consistency as "Cognitive Resonance." When the behaviors don't match, there is inconsistency. We call this "Cognitive Dissonance." These inconsistent actions create the potential for mistrust with your audiences.

1   Look at your values and style attributes and assess how well you are living up to how your brand currently lives and emulate them. Please refer to the definitions you created for each in Module 1. There will always be opportunities or gaps for improvement.

2   List each of your core values and style attributes in the left column below. In the right column, rate how consistent you are in living each value and style attribute.

Step 1 - Rate Personal Brand Presence Attributes

VALUE	**Rate Consistency in Living My Value** 1=Never 2=Occasionally 3=Frequently 4=Almost Always 5=Always

STYLE	**Rate Consistency in Living My STYLE** 1=Never 2=Occasionally 3=Frequently 4=Almost Always 5=Always

STEP 2: Now here is the first step to creating alignment and building your Personal Brand Presence!

Select the one attribute from each category (Value & Style) with the lowest number. Identify at least one or two behaviors/actions you will take to elevate your alignment with that attribute daily/weekly/or monthly and identify a reasonable time span to accomplish each.

- **Value:** _____

Action:	Timing: When will I apply it?

- **Style:** _____

Action:	Timing: When will I apply it?

Note: *You could do this action exercise with every one of your Value and Style attributes to outline how you would start consciously making your attributes much more tangible in your experiences.*

Building Your Personal Brand Vocabulary

As part of building your brand through a multi-dimensional fashion, our vocabulary plays a huge role in how we can articulate our thoughts, ideas, and position on world views. This activity will help you become more familiar with terms that are in alignment with your DNA attributes and help you to speak your authentic self more clearly and precisely. You can use these terms in any way to enhance your narrative.

LIST YOUR **CORE VALUES** horizontally *ACROSS* THE PAGE DIRECTLY BELOW: Then identify up to five additional terms that reflect (synonymous) with the **MEANING** of the core value you listed above it.

_____	_____	_____	_____
(list synonyms below)	(list synonyms below)	(list synonyms below)	(list synonyms below)
_____	_____	_____	_____
_____	_____	_____	_____
_____	_____	_____	_____
_____	_____	_____	_____

LIST YOUR **BRAND STYLE attributes** horizontally *ACROSS* THE PAGE DIRECTLY BELOW: Then identify up to five additional terms that reflect (synonymous) with the **MEANING** of the core value you listed above it.

_____	_____	_____	_____
(list synonyms below)	(list synonyms below)	(list synonyms below)	(list synonyms below)
_____	_____	_____	_____
_____	_____	_____	_____
_____	_____	_____	_____
_____	_____	_____	_____

CHAPTER 7 | EXERCISE 6

Bonus!
Advertising Checklist

Use these points to check your advertising messages prior to disseminating to your market.

ADVERTISING EFFECTIVENESS CHECKPOINTS:

- Does your ad clearly identify your brand position verbally & visually (immediately & throughout the ad)?
- Does your ad clearly communicate your brand's unique "WHY?"
- Does the ad feature a tag line that reinforces the brand's OVERALL BENEFIT?
- Is the ad's tone, voice, and style true to your brand's essence and style/personality?
- Is there something about your ad that makes the reader admire and relate to your personal brand?
- Is the ad as simple and clear (uncomplicated) as possible around the offer/message?
- Does your ad reveal your "Why" and connect with the reader on an emotional level? (*Does it win the reader's heart or capture his/her imagination?*)
- Is your ad significantly, visually different from that of your competitors (*does it reflect your brand Style*)?
- Does your ad reinforce the core value(s) of your brand?
- Does the ad inspire your target market to act? (*What is your call to action—CTA?*)

- Does your ad use brand-relevant vocabulary that speaks consistently about who you are?

- Is your ad so powerful that it has the potential to keep your competitors awake a night worrying about your brand?

- Does your ad highlight quantifiable differentiators that sets you apart from the competition?

- Can your competitor make the same exact claim?

- Does the ad make the reader to feel they would be better off by having interacted with your brand?

- Do you have a process to consistently manage the positive reaction and serve each customer to the fullest of your brand "WHY?"

- Do you have a way to track/measure where your market is seeing and responding to your ad?

- Do you have a process in place to nurture the new clients you get from the ad well beyond initial contact and sales?

- If this ad doesn't generate the results you want, what will you do next?

ONLINE RESOURCES:

*Personal Brand Presence DNA Onesheet template - PDF:
https://bit.ly/2O2CBNW

*What is Personal Branding? - BrandByte #9 video:
https://youtu.be/sZ5WvNuSDx0

*Brand Mini Workshops Link Resource:
https://bit.ly/3gmT5g5

*Brand Values and Style Attributes Client Video:
https://bit.ly/3f3dsPb

*For a variety of client mantras and how they leverage them, take a look at this video: *https://bit.ly/2ZnxyNg*

*Video example of a client experiencing the power of her Personal Brand Mantra: *https://bit.ly/31Bs04u*

*You can purchase a download of *The 6 Myths of Small Business Branding* **ebook and workbook at:**
https://bit.ly/38ix3rJ

* Personal Brand Alignment - BrandByte #11 video:
https://youtu.be/p_3z4oBJefE

*Watch excerpt of webinar for case study examples of clients leveraging their Personal Brand Presence:
https://bit.ly/3geA538

My Daily Personal Brand Declarations List: page 122

ADDITIONAL SUPPLEMENTAL RESOURCE TOOL:
Ignite Your Personal Brand Presence DNA - Online Course:
www.PersonalBrandPresence.com - Complete Video Module + Workbook Course

"Your greatest healing would be to wake up from what we are not."

- Mooji

———

"It takes a lot of energy to be a person. It takes no energy to BE yourself."

- Mooji

———

ABOUT THE AUTHOR

Suzanne Tulien is the cofounder of Brand Ascension, an experiential consulting and training firm that works with organizations & solopreneurs to achieve transformational and sustainable Brand success through strategic internal Brand defining and aligning practices. As pioneer of the Brand defining methodology —Brand DNA (Dimensional Nucleic Assets®) and the Brand DNA Journey™—she has helped numerous small, to medium-sized businesses create consistent, relevant, and distinctive experiences that engage, inspire, and win their employees and customers for life; not to mention position their Brands for extraordinary growth.

She is author of three books: *Brand DNA, Personal Brand Clarity*, and *The 6 Myths of Small Business Branding*. Her goal is to clarify the client Brand's value position and guide them to walk their talk and deliver on their promise every time.

In 2011, Suzanne reengineered her Business Brand DNA methodology to support the solopreneurs of the world and engage them into becoming more conscious, strategic, and deliberate in assigning deep meaning to their own Personal Brands as they show up in their business. Since then, she has been running Personal Brand Presence masterminds, workshops, and speaking and training. In 2020, Suzanne launched a comprehensive online course, "Ignite Your Personal Brand Presence DNA," to help the solo-professional identify, define, and align themselves to realize their unique distinction and ultimate competitive advantage to live their potential from the inside out.

As a certified trainer in experiential and accelerated adult-learning methodologies, BA delivers highly effective Brand consulting and facilitation sessions onsite, online (virtual web-based), and on demand that engage the different learning styles and ways humans process information: Auditory, visual, kinesthetic, and intellectual. Her techniques maximize and ensure each person's contribution to the Brand-building process. This approach transfers the discovery and understanding of the critical elements of a Brand that make the business unique and supports the overall strategic positioning of the Brand as part of the organization's core business strategy.

CONTACT AND SERVICES INFORMATION:
SOCIAL MEDIA PRESENCE:

- LinkedIn: linkedin.com/in/suzannetulien
- Facebook: www.Facebook.com/BrandAscension
- Instagram: www.Instagram.com/BrandAscension

CORE SERVICES/PRODUCTS:
- **Brand Positioning Assessment Tools** – a comprehensive set of self-assessment tools in areas such as Customer Service, Brand Behavior, Visual Brand, Branded Website, Employee Assessment, etc.
- **Internal Brand Development** - Brand DNA Discovery Process and Implementation for businesses with employees.
- **Brand Awareness Events** – Induction of Employees into the Brand DNA
- **Internal Brand Integration and On-Brand Employee Engagement**
- **Ignite Your Personal Brand Presence DNA - Online Course** - for the solo-professional - www.PersonalBrandPresence.com
- **Brand Training/Consulting** – [workshops + webinars]
- **Personal Brand Leadership Coachin**g – Group and Private
- **Speaker Brand Coaching/Training** – Group and Private
- **Speaking/Training** – Keynotes, Breakouts
- Three Books: *Brand DNA, Personal Brand Clarity, 6 Myths of Small Business Branding*
- Graphic Design/Brand Story/PR *(Brand DNA graduate clients only)*

TARGET MARKETS: Internationally (English-speaking)
- **Business Brand DNA:** Small to middle-market sized companies with five to 1,500 employees who are passionate about differentiation and living their "why/promise/mission' through alignment of their employees, processes, and

leadership strategy.
- **Personal Brand Presence:** solo-professionals (real estate agents/brokers, consultants, coaches, authors, practitioners, speakers), and emerging leaders/managers and sales teams within organizations who want to step into their full potential through self-actualization.
- **Speaking/Training:** Business associations and conferences whose members are CXO decision-makers *(globally)* and desire to deepen the connection with their own Brand to their internal culture, external community, & their prospective markets.

Identify. Define. Align. Suzanne Tulien is a Brand Clarity Expert, specializing in identifying and defining distinctive Brand positioning through her proprietary process, to achieve extreme clarity on her clients' unique differentiation, master consistencies to build trust, and create "on-brand" actions and behaviors from the inside out. She is the author of three books: *Brand DNA*, *Personal Brand Clarity*, and *The 6 Myths of Small Business Branding*. She speaks, trains, and consults internationally.

Visit: **www.BrandAscension.com**

> *"I highly recommend Suzanne Tulien's **Personal Brand Clarity** book for solo-professionals who know they have expertise and want to carve out their distinction in big ways. As a Travel Adventure Specialist, going through her process was transformational because it created a level of awareness that is undeniable, reaffirmed my own truer beliefs about myself, and provided the narrative for me to begin living it even more. My clients and prospects took notice and started referring me more because they better understood my value! This book and process is a must for solopreneurs!"* **—Phoenix Sagen,** CEO, MyTravel4Ever Travel Agency

"Tapping into my Personal Brand's "Why" was the crescendo of this process for me. With this newfound clarity, I have been able to be more confident and intentional with my messaging and branding, align my narrative and tone, and attract the perfect clients who resonate with who I am This book and its exercises are like the golden keys that help us unlock our potential, when it comes to really stepping into who we are on a deeper level. I have truly enjoyed this transformative process, and find it so effortless to create content from this place of true being and essence. The words flow with ease and I know I will connect with the right people, just by being me. Thank you Suzanne!"
— **Crystal Blue,** Owner, Blue Zen Center

"Going through this process of identifying, defining and aligning to my Personal Brand Presence enabled me to start taking more control over the perceptions others had of me and my business. Personal Brand Clarity, unleashed the clarity to represent what I stand for and am able to discern differently towards my own alignment on a daily basis. I am now attracting people, great clients, and more 'on-brand' situations. It is a powerfully transformational growth process and I recommend it to every solopreneur and leader!" — **Dianna Dalton-Daily**, Realtor, The Platinum Group

Made in the USA
Monee, IL
26 October 2020

45833364R00115